Do Not Forget Me Street
Remembering the Budapesti Schindlers

Erica Frydenberg

In memory of the victims of the Bondi Hanukkah massacre, 14th December 2025, and the heroes who risked their own lives to save others

Do Not Forget Me Street
Copyright©2026 Erica Frydenberg
Print ISBN: 978-1-76109-729-4
Ebook ISBN: 978-1-76109-730-0
Cover design: by Graham Davidson
Cover photo supplied by Erica Frydenberg
All efforts have been made to seek permission or otherwise acknowledge copyright ownership of photos not belonging to the Frydenberg family. However, the publisher welcomes related advice and will seek to attribute copyright as required in this regard.

First published 2026 by
GINNINDERRA PRESS
PO Box 2 Bentleigh 3204
ginninderrapress.com.au

Contents

Prologue   5

Part 1

Chapter One: Born into Chaos   11
    A near miss   11
Chapter Two: Budapest: Beauty, and the Beast   20
    Spinoza Cafe   22
    The Dohány Street Synagogue   26
Chapter Three: Who Were the Magyars?   30
    The Ghetto of Budapest   40
Chapter Four: Nándor   46
    The Memorial Museum of Hungarian Speaking Jewry   50
    Grandchildren as historians   54

Part 2

Chapter Five: One Budapesti Schindler   65
    Carl Lutz   65
    The country boy   70
    Stepping into the Glass House   74
    The bombings began   80
    How the diplomatic passes came into being   83
    The Fall of the Glass House   87
Chapter Six: Schindler meets Kasztner   93
    Risk without glory   94
    The journalist who saw it coming   98
    Kasztner comes to Budapest   101
    When the Germans came to town   103
    Bartering for lives; blood for goods   106
Chapter Seven: Raoul Wallenberg: Another Budapesti Schindler   112
    The hundredth birthday celebrations   114
    Who gets credit for what?   116

The thrill of a find	118
Farkas—The man with Wallenberg	122
Doctor and patient	127
Chapter Eight: House of Terror and Those Shoes	129
House of Terror	129
Shoes on the Bank of the Danube	132
Arrow Cross Stories	136

Part 3

Chapter 9: In Australia	147
The Sydney Chevra Kadisha	147
Getting out	150
In Sydney	153
Meeting George Farkas	157
Chapter 10: Death of Kasztner and the Birth of Israel	164
She came my way	172
Új Kelet: The Messenger	174

Part 4

Chapter 11: Philosophy, psychology and silence	181
The dignity of silence: Braham-Eichel-Farkas	184
Jews rescuing Jews	185
Long silences	186
Family secrets	190
Survivor guilt	191
Coping, resilience and fortitude	191
A legacy of hope and purpose	200

Prologue

In September 2024, eight women sit around a table reflecting on the book that they had just read: *The Piano Player of Budapest*. It is a powerful story told by Roxanne De Bastion about her grandfather's survival in the war years in Budapest, and as a 'foreigner' in the English town of Stratford-upon-Avon. She is a third-generation survivor who tells the story of endurance, migration and a country once left, never to be revisited. She pieces together the Holocaust memoir from recordings and family photographs, complemented by interviews and research.

During the informal book club discussion, four of the women (myself included), lamented how little we knew of our family stories. Each of our parents had survived the Holocaust in Budapest, but in the main, the parents had remained silent about their wartime experiences. We did not have the good fortune to have recorded testimony to draw upon, and our families' photo collections from that period were scant. Yet as I have become keenly curious in my adult years about our family's past and identity, in the era of privileged travel and the internet, I try to fill in the many blanks that remain.

There is a desire among many of us to understand the nature of our origins, the world of the generation that came before us; a keen curiosity to understand the past, and a willingness to learn from it. Looking retrospectively from our current times and circumstances, can help us appreciate what came before—even if we have to join the dots or make some assumptions. After all, we were not there. We go beyond the self to embrace others who may no longer be here, and as we do just that, in a virtual sense, it brings a sense of consolation and sometimes closure.

I wanted to understand survival, the immigrant experience and the will to help others at all costs. My uncle Nandor was one such figure in my life who never talked about his wartime experiences, and that, more than anything, raised my curiosity. There was mystery in the silence that surrounded someone who had hero status in the lives of my family, but there was little hard evidence about his wartime activities. What was a family myth in a child's eyes needed some verification for me as an adult.

As I embarked on this personal journey into my family's history, I became increasingly aware of the challenges in traversing that kaleidoscopic landscape where there is much to discover, absorb and lament. Despite the difficulty of connecting with these bygone worlds, both in an emotional and a practical way, there remains the ongoing opportunity to gain insights into the past as best we can. The discovery of past worlds and the lives of survivors can be powerfully instructive for us.

In my quest to research my own family history, I see through a lens that is most familiar to me—that of a psychologist, where questions are asked not just about the *what was* but also the *why*. The reader can also ask those questions, and while the answers are not always clear, it is inevitable that both myself, as the writer, and you, as the reader, continue to learn and potentially find satisfaction in the revelations of what the past can teach us today.

While motives may not always be evident, and emotions may only be guessed at, we think about human capacity and capability, and at times find ourselves in awe of those ancestors who preceded us. If we fail to be moved to admiration, we might nevertheless be challenged by some of the ethical dilemmas that history throws up. We can always learn and grow in discovery—better to know than not to know—even as we access first-hand accounts of unimaginable horrors, recorded for the explicit purpose of remembrance.

As we live our lives today and as we travel to places of exquisite beauty and explore with curiosity and enthusiasm, it is important to be reminded that there is a past—and a present which should not be accepted without question. The past helps us to understand the present, examined through our own personal, as well as evidential, lens.

The uncontrollable world of yesterday can be contrasted to what is around us, and out of control today. How one stays sane, keeps perspective, and tries to live a good life remains as important today as it ever was. I begin my walk in the shoes of others.

Part 1

'Gratitude is the parent of all virtues.'

—Marcus Tullius Cicero

Chapter One
Born into Chaos

There is street in Budapest called *Nefelejcs utca*—Do Not Forget Me Street. In English it sounds lovely, bucolic, peaceful. It has a pleading ring to it in the Hungarian language — *Nefelejcs utca*. It does not want to be left or forgotten.[1]

It's a name that I cannot help saying under my breath a dozen times while I consider its implications.

When was this street named? What were those who named it thinking? Did they imagine that there would be residents who would one day be rounded up and driven from their homes and birthplace; who would have to go into hiding; who would have to make a choice to leave in search of a better life? To choose between the threat of persecution in the now, and an uncertain and dangerous future?

In real terms, it is a very ordinary street with an extraordinary name in a not-so-ordinary city. It was a street I frequently visited as a child, during the horrific first years of my life, when the Holocaust consumed Europe, coming, finally, to the place of my birth.

Budapest has been described as the Paris of the East, conjuring up visions of beauty and romance. Like some European cities, it has had a chequered history, distinguished by culture and beauty, as well as occupation, terror and violence. It was at Budapest's nadir of violence and persecution towards Jews that I was born to a Hungarian Jewish family, amidst the chaos of war.

A near miss

I was born on 5 October 1943 in Budapest, the beautiful capital of Hungary, where most members of our small family lived in the heart of the city. War raged in Europe in the first half of the 1940s, but until around the time my mother began to carry me, Budapest was spared some of the horrors devastating much of Europe. While harsh legal edicts against the Jews of Hungary were mounting, the Holocaust and the Nazi regime's 'Final Solution' had not yet engulfed Budapest.

Life seemed still to be manageable for Jewish families like mine. When the time came for me to be born, my mother, out of pride, or pragmatism, or a mixture of the two, decided on a Budapest hospital as the place to have her child. My parents spent the first years of their married life living with my father's parents in the Strausz family compound in the town of Makó in the onion district of Hungary.

Moreover, a few months after my birth, I was taken to the Mosoly Albuma photographic studios to have an official baby portrait taken. The picture, a monochrome photograph of a smiling infant, is much like any portrait organised by proud new parents of the day. (I still have the portrait, some eight decades later). As a document of regular middle-class European life, it speaks to the apparent normality of the scene and the tenuous peace that lay over Budapest that year, 1943. It holds no clues to the chaos that was about to unfold.

Shortly after that picture was taken, the rising tide of fascism in Hungary led to closer cooperation between the Hungarian and Nazi governments. The rights of Jewish people were curtailed, slowly; and then all at once, and circumstances changed quickly.

On 19 March 1944, the German tanks rolled into Budapest. And on 21 March Adolph Eichmann[2] set himself up briefly at the Astoria Hotel in the heart of the city, before moving to the Majestic Hotel on Sváb Hill. The wearing of the yellow star and ghettoisation began. Chaos descended on all the city's inhabitants, especially the Jews and the Romas.[3]

Families like mine were ousted from their homes and forced to take shelter in underground basements alongside hundreds and sometimes thousands of others. Our family ended up in the basement of a Swiss protectorate house with many other displaced Jewish families. Above ground the bombs were falling. Hygiene was minimal and levels of distress were high. An environment where a crying infant could cause pandemonium was no place for a baby.

In the mayhem of war, parents will do whatever it takes for their child to survive. The conditions in the basement were so unsuitable for an infant that my mother must have had to make the difficult decision to move me into one of several Red Cross homes for babies and young children. She must have been convinced that leaving me in the care of the Red Cross ensured my best chance of survival.

And that is where I spent some months of the first year of my life as war raged through Budapest, and the rest of my family hid underneath it.

It was part of family lore that one dark night, my mother had a premonition that something terrible was going to happen to me in the Red Cross home. She convinced my uncle Nándor, a man with considerable connections with the local constabulary, to intervene.

He was given permission to go out with my mother after the nightly curfew. Fortunately, they had the security of a car and a bodyguard. They reached the Red Cross house, knocked on the door and asked to collect me.

The gruff and suspicious attendant told them that all the children had been evacuated to the countryside in anticipation of a likely bombing. My mother and uncle were not convinced, particularly as they could hear crying inside. The attendant explained that the children she could hear wailing had been too sick to be moved and were unlikely to survive the night.

The stand-off was resolved when Nándor and my mother forced their way in and soon found me in a cot, frail and wailing but not, as the Red Cross attendant had insisted, evacuated to the country, nor at death's door. They swiftly bundled me up and took me back to the Swiss protectorate house.

My sister Judy recalls that, upon my return, I was weak and immobile. Even though I was almost one year old, I was unable to walk or even crawl, and my reactions seemed slow and dull. I was malnourished and had certainly failed to thrive in the children's home.

Our family remained in that basement home for the next few months until the end of the war. Above ground, the food stores were being bombed so we sheltered in the basement with so many others. We were packed like sardines, hunger was a permanent state, which my sister remembers to this day. With the help and protection of the Swiss government, and thanks largely to Nándor's intervention and ongoing assistance, we managed to survive, not only for the remainder of the war, but through the difficult years to follow.

My family, proud Hungarians despite everything, continued to stay in Budapest. It is a city that has lost and regained its lustre over the decades. It is a city divided by the Danube River which once ran red with the blood of victims of Hungary's home-grown fascists who terrorised the population. Today that river is the highly popular route for cruises that start in Budapest and end up in Amsterdam, or vice versa—a busy river straddled by its 15 bridges and the bustling life on either side. This was the beautiful capital of a country that people like my parents ultimately left behind, never looking back but resolutely moving forward.

It was much later that I learned the reasons for their leaving. It was not in 1945 when the Germans had left, after their attempts at *dejudification*, and not after the reign of terror from the Arrow Cross—the fascist group who were tried by the people after the war, and in many cases executed—but when the Communists took power. The Communist regime set about transforming the country in ways that people found unacceptable, confiscating businesses and properties, and eliminating autonomy and religious practice. This was the final straw for my parents. It was 1949, and this time, people could anticipate what was in store for them: diminishing personal rights and freedoms and an intolerance of religious practice.

Five years after war's end, and after much turmoil and travel through Europe into France, we emigrated to Australia and landed in the beautiful harbour city of Sydney.

An enchanted life followed. I grew up in a rapidly changing world. A happy childhood in Bondi, tertiary education including studying with Germaine Greer, a career in psychology, London in the swinging 60s, marriage, children and grandchildren.

I spent sixteen happy years in Bondi, somewhat disconnected from the experiences of my parents, their family and friends. We just lived our lives as a family: three daughters attending the local primary school, a father coping with ill health, and a mother who did it all. My mother was the carer, running the belt manufacturing enterprise in the kitchen which was a factory by day and an eatery by night. There was a little socialising and efforts to keep in touch with a few intimates, friends from the home country and friendships made on the ship during the long journey to our new home. The past and where we came from were not topics that were discussed with us or within earshot of others. Perhaps it was too painful; looking back was not helpful in coping with the present. There was always the pressure of adaptation and day-to-day survival in our new country.

Despite the challenges experienced by my immigrant parents, a good life was lived which would not have happened without my uncle Nándor's courage. My life was full and busy through the 20th century and the early years of the 21st century. I had no special interest in history until it came time to look back and introduce my children to their past. This was a world they did not know, and of which I knew too little.

Later in life I reflected on this time, on my origins, and on the context in which I was born, and in which my parents and their Budapesti[4] friends and family lived and survived. I wanted to know more about this earlier world and, in particular about Nándor, as I was aware that he was instrumental in saving my life. As a man, I found Nándor to be capable, softly spoken, and someone who knew his mind. He had a way of letting you know what he wanted from you: a suggestion became more of a must-do. He was intriguing in his confidence and had the means to get what he wanted—or was that just his determination?

I felt increasingly drawn to explore the story of my family's survival and the people who made it possible. As I recorded my own story, I learned of many others and felt compelled to explore further.

I had tried to draw Nándor out on his memories of Budapest and wartime experiences, and I always came away disappointed. He evaded my questions artfully—he was eloquent and polite but gave little away.

It wasn't until a later chance conversation much later in life that I began to understand the full extent of Nándor's secret life in wartime Budapest.

I grew curious about my uncle's careful silence around his role in Budapest. I began to investigate, and little by little began to discover clues that suggested that Nándor had used his influence to rescue many more Jewish people in wartime Budapest than merely me.

The dramatic story of how my uncle Nándor had saved my life became a well-known part of family legend, a touchstone that highlighted the strength of my mother's intuition and the resourcefulness and indomitable will of my uncle Nándor.

Many people, known and unknown, owe their lives to Nándor's bravery—I am just one of them. Hundreds more Jewish families may have been saved by him and men like him.

I became interested in Nándor and others like him, strong, determined men who risked it all and saved others. Good men in bad times, some celebrated, others with more chequered reputations, and others just silent achievers.

Every new fact I discovered about Nándor brought with it new questions. His actions in resisting fascism and saving the lives of the persecuted were objectively heroic. So why did he never speak of them?

It was not uncommon for Holocaust survivors to avoid speaking of those events due to the lingering trauma borne by those memories, but that alone doesn't seem reason enough for Nándor's stoicism. Later in life, more survivors began to speak—with support groups, to collectors of oral and written testimonies, and to place their experiences on record for Yad Vashem, Israel's official Holocaust memorial museum, which began to collect testimonials for perpetuity.

With the passing of years, there was a growing awareness of the Holocaust and the stories of the survivors. First, the high-profile prosecution at Nuremberg of Nazi war criminals, followed by a generation of influential Jewish filmmakers and artists who grappled with the legacy of the Shoah.

Oskar Schindler is possibly the most well-known of those people who risked their own lives to save the Jewish civilians of Europe, although there were many more active at that time. Some are written into the history books. Others have slipped from them, into the silent streets of memory.

Schindler, the German industrialist, used his power and wealth to save many lives and was designated as Righteous Amongst the Nations by Yad Vashem, and immortalised in Thomas Keneally's novel *Schindler's Ark*, and Steven Spielberg's movie adaptation *Schindler's List*.

He is rightly remembered as a hero for his actions. But in a post-*Schindler's List* world, why would other men who walked similar paths choose that their actions be forgotten? Who are these lesser-known or unknown heroes, and why did they cultivate silence?

There are answers to be found. I look to a circle of men who moved in the same circles in Budapest in the 1940s, working quietly and swiftly with foreign ambassadors and influential Nazis, acting as quasi ambassadors themselves, with cars, security and the freedom to move around beyond curfews.

They engaged in extraordinary work to save thousands of lives under threat in the chaos of war. My uncle Nándor was just one of these forgotten figures.

This book is an attempt to tell his story—to reckon with the silence of both the man, Nándor, and the silence of the years. To tell his story—and those of other men: Carl Lutz—the courageous Swiss diplomat; János (John) Farkas—a

Hungarian freedom fighter, hero among Holocaust survivors and the right-hand man of the well-known Raoul Wallenberg, the Swedish diplomat who saved thousands of Jewish lives. These were the lesser-known, or totally forgotten 'Secret Schindlers' of Budapest. In Hungarian, we would call them the '*Budapesti Schindlers*'.

Despite my family connection, I was unaware of the full extent of these men's actions until a revelation in later life set me on a mission to discover as much as I could. With every new piece of the puzzle I found came new questions. Nándor and János Farkas were lifelong friends who rebuilt their lives in Sydney and kept their secrets between them.

Why did they never speak of their wartime heroism? Were they just doing what was expected? Or were their brave encounters and amazing feats simply not recognised in their new homes? Does their own silence—or the silence about them—bring to light much bigger questions? Are those who stay silent more likely to be safe? Are those close to home generally the least celebrated? Does it pay to be in the shadows rather than pay a high price for being in the public eye? Is trauma a key player, or does survivor guilt play a powerful role?

Why were Nándor and the other '*Budapesti Schindlers*' silent about their actions? Fear of reprisal? Of persecution for their actions in the morally complex reality of saving lives from the Nazi death machine? What occurred in wartime Budapest that made these men so reticent to remember or to be remembered?

These questions sit heavily with me, for both my personal connection to Nándor and his circles, and as a psychologist and student of human nature. What kept these men silent? What can we observe about human nature from their decision to disappear from recorded history? How are trauma, resilience, and silence connected?

So began a journey to uncover the stories of these men and the ambassadors they worked with as they moved from Budapest to postwar Tel Aviv and Jerusalem, and the harbour city, Sydney, on that most southern continent.

Where did those stories intersect? What and who played a part in the men's fate? Did silence help at least some of them to live a good life in Australia? To me, their stories highlight the possible purpose and value for those who chose to stay silent.

The virtue of doing good and staying in the shadows without recognitions or accolades is the common thread that binds together the stories of at least two of these '*Budapesti Schindlers*'.

And in some ways that thread binds me too, as an infant of the Holocaust and child of survivors. It is one of the eternal tragedies of human nature—that we delay asking questions of our forebears in a timely fashion, and so the great silence that submerges our understanding of ourselves deepens with the passing years. This is the story of the attempt to break that silence, and the start of a journey to find the important remnants of the past.

I do this with a strong sense of gratitude for those who saved my family and countless others. Gratitude is an appreciation of the other that gives a return in satisfaction and joy through its expression. It is a keystone in what makes us happy, helps us to cultivate relationships and helps us to appreciate what is good in our lives. In the words of Marcus Tullius Cicero, the Roman philosopher: 'Gratitude is not only the greatest of virtues, but the parent of all others.'

Chapter Two
Budapest: Beauty, and the Beast

In 2023, some three-quarters of a century after emigrating, my husband and I, along with our children and five grandchildren, go as a family to Budapest. I walk the streets and think about the fantasies I grew up with, of the great beauty of Budapest and the repression of the Soviet years. I make comparisons with the dreariness of the Communist era visit of the 1970s and today. I set out to enjoy and to understand. Do Not Forget Me Street is my first port of call. The street symbolises why I am here: to remember and not to forget.

Memory is an interesting and all-important phenomenon. With aging, one remembers the past more vividly and makes fewer imprints of the present. But the past is an inexact science. History is made up of fact, memory, and some conjecture. As not all the facts are known we use our imagination to fill in the gaps and sometimes colour the images. I may well be doing this by traversing back eight decades to reconcile with the present, and to find a way to enhance the future. My journey is a personalised historical search of discovery, recorded as best I can, and if there are facts to be corrected, others may be able to assist.

Budapest 2023 does not disappoint. It is a beautiful buzzing metropolis with claims to some of the most exquisite sites and edifices in Europe. The Parliament House is the most magnificent I have seen in size, scope and structure with symbolism everywhere you look. Commenced in 1885, it took eleven years to complete. The building is replete with art and sculpture, and like much of Budapest, at every turn tells a story.

We eat together each night—one night in a modern restaurant called Meshuga. The literal translation of this Yiddish word 'meshuga' is 'crazy'. And it *is* a crazy meal. Playful, modern cuisine, a crazy mix of tastes and textures. The food is interesting, a fusion of Israeli and Mediterranean cuisine and nothing is quite what you would expect. The restaurant, like many things in Budapest, has a reality just below the surface. Beauty, culture, some contemporary world dilemmas as well as a past to contend with.

It is outside Meshuga that we had our favourite photo of Budapest taken, impromptu, not dressed in our best but smiling nevertheless as we were leaving the light-hearted, confusing 21st century restaurant.

Our smiles reflect our happiness in the moment and sit in tandem with sadness. As psychologists, we know that it is possible to experience two emotions simultaneously, the happiness of the moment and the realisation that we are treading the path of those who experienced the hardship and pain of Budapest, 1944-1945.

On our return to Australia I am gifted a photo album of our memorable trip to Budapest. The book is replete with beautiful images, but on the cover is a happy, casual impromptu photo of the family outside the restaurant bearing the name, Meshuga. We just look happy.

And on reflection, the restaurant represents what Budapest is today: good-natured, good-humoured, now accepting of its Jewish population but less so of immigrants and refugees from places of poverty and despair in other parts of the world. It is also the site of countless atrocities—to Jews and gentiles alike, spanning the decades of my life and the centuries before it.

There are many different Budapests to write about. A decade is not long in the history of a city, and the first half of a decade, even less. Yet the city can still mirror much of what went on in the turbulent years of the 1940s.

It was the city in which I and my two sisters were born. My mother chose to give birth to all her three daughters in the metropolis of Budapest, thus hoping to imbue a pedigree and status to each child through the location of their birth. A small, unremarkable onion-growing town 200 kilometres from Budapest 'would just not do'.

I could have called this book *Beauty and the Beast*—it is a story about beautiful Budapest, the place of culture and progress where I learned of the lives of my family in the 1930s and the 1940s. But the beast reared its proverbial head in the fraught years of the 1940s in Budapest—not that life for Jewish Hungarians before 1940 was easy, but my family seemed to be doing well.

Spinoza Cafe

29 June 2023: We spend our first night gathered in Budapest at the Spinoza Café. It appears in the stories of 1940s Budapest as a bakery. It is located at the border of what was then the Jewish Ghetto and is known for welcoming guests for a traditional meal after the synagogue service. We chose it as our first night venue to get into the spirit of Budapest. There is a piano standing ready for cabarets and concerts, and for us, the pianist plays any song of our choosing. As a finale he plays 'Happy Birthday'—the children order dessert with a candle and sing 'happy birthday' even though my birthday was some six months away. The family sang along in English, and I found I could not remember the words in Hungarian—most probably because I had not heard it sung in that language. We were not a family to celebrate birthdays or anything much for that matter.

But for me today, there is pure joy in sharing the visit to my roots with my family, to see everyone smiling and laughing as they exchange humorous stories about me. There is no trace of a horror-filled past in their experiences. In fact, I wear a white t-shirt bought in Melbourne with the word 'Happiness' embroidered on it. I didn't need to remind myself to be happy, but wanted to symbolically share the satisfaction of the experience. to accentuate that my true happiness is the joy of family.

But then there are mixed emotions to come when we are confronted with the realities of the past and the homes my family inhabited; why they had to leave and with what emotions—certainly with minimal baggage. Who lives in their dwellings now? And do they ever consider the history that brought them to their lodgings?

On the last Friday in June 2023, we commence our pilgrimage to former family apartments. On the way we visit Klauzál Tér. These days it is just a locality within an inner urban setting, but in the winter of 1944-1945, 'mountains of frozen corpses were piled high'. It was well within the confines of what was the Budapest Ghetto, where there were too many corpses and nowhere to bury them. Today it is like a comfortable inner urban location where perhaps young people prefer to live, rather than those in the middle years who hanker for green grass and a more serene lifestyle.

We visit the family apartments. It was not easy to locate the resident of Klauzál Tér 13, so we first entered the adjacent apartment, now a small Airbnb; so 21st century!

The building is typical of Budapest and many European apartments of its period, with an entrance marked by a heavy timber door painted green, just big enough for us to enter. There are several panels higher than the door framed above with a semi-circular arc, 10 feet or so, decorated with panels of glass. One of those panels had been struck by a projectile, a stray throw or perhaps intentional vandalism, as happens in many inner urban areas. Inside the central courtyard it is as I remember: a typical Budapesti apartment building. We entered the Airbnb by arrangement, and as you would expect for a rental, it is clean and well-kept, but not flash. The cleaners were just leaving as we arrived. That apartment raised no emotional reaction from any of us. It failed to tell its story.

However, we must have been a noisy lot. The resident of the very apartment we had been trying to gain access to must have been stirred by our presence and greeted us—shirtless on the hot day, and we received a fulsome welcome to come in and hear his story.

The man had been living there for many years, taking it over from someone who had lived there since 1945. He had lived there with his wife but recently lost his partner to ill health. The kitchen was a modest affair—a man looking after himself.

His name was Dávid Szöllősi and he was an author, indeed a poet, with walls lined floor-to-ceiling with books. He generously gifted us with a self-authored book of poetry, *Csak rímszerész vagyok…* translated to *I Am Only a Rhyme Maker*. He seemed like a truly deep and generous man who did not take himself too seriously, as is suggested by the title of his book.

Dávid told us that he had been a collector of *National Geographic*. The first edition came out, with pictures, in 1905. He proudly pointed to his collection which took up one wall fully stacked with these volumes. No one bothered to clarify how and when he started to gather these magazines, or ask what was the first valuable volume on his bookshelf? One obvious question that came to mind was, 'Did he enjoy vicarious travel experiences through his *National Geographics*?' During the four decades of Communist rule it would have been the best option for international travel available to him.

There was not too much room for sleeping—a fold-out couch seemed to be adequate; there were beautiful parquetry floors, and bookshelves on every wall. The apartment was spacious enough but would have been much grander before the carve-up of the Communist era, when no one had the luxury of a multi-bedroom dwelling for one or two persons.

I saw my grandparents and my parents and a little of myself in that apartment where we spent holidays and landed for refuge, as Jews were being rounded up in the countryside. What were the family conversations? Joyful holiday chatter, and later, when the family came for shelter during the time of roundups in rural Hungary, relief and anguish. There must have been conversations of fear and dread, perhaps in hushed tones, as everyone was under suspicion.

Both my grandparents, my family and extended family went into hiding as bombs and terror reigned during the rugged months in the second half of 1944. There would have been conversations of relief at war's end when the grandparents returned to their home. Were their possessions intact? Had anyone plundered their apartment the way others have described a return to ransacked apartments emptied of possessions? There must have been conversations about what to take and what to leave behind when the family made their final flight from the city, and perhaps some relief and gratitude if their home remained intact on their return. Perhaps good people had safeguarded their possessions. Neither I nor my siblings nor cousins recall talk of plunder and destruction in the family home.

There was much to contemplate as one looked back from the comfort of a tourist's eye in the 21st century.

Did the family see what was coming their way? Or did they continue with the general complacency of the Jews of Budapest? Did they think that what was happening in Poland, Slovakia, or the Ukraine was never going to happen in Hungary? The war was nearly over, and any day sanity would return, the liberating Allied armies would land, and the Nazis would be banished.

That was likely to have been the tenor of the conversations. And after all, Nándor, the man who could talk to those in high places as well as to the man on the street, the man who could do anything, the man who was so well connected, would always be able to keep us safe. And there was always optimism, and always prayer, particularly for those with a religious bent like my family.

The questions and the emotions were running high in Klauzál Tér. After all, we are in the midst of what had been the Budapest Ghetto. A short distance from Klazál Tér, we find ourselves in the street that was not to be forgotten.

We arrive at Nefelejcs utca 50, the home of my uncle Nándor. We enter through two solid timber gates with glass panels protected by iron grids, just as one would have in any inner urban area that needed security and protection. Interestingly, Nándor's home in Sydney was protected by similar grids. The gates here have an additional touch of daisy-like metal flowers for decoration.

We enter that now-familiar European-style apartment block with a central courtyard brought to life with foliage. The courtyard area was not one suited for kicking a football, but rather had two benches for sitting and relaxing. A space designed for feeling safe and secure. Not a feeling shared by Jews in mid-1940s Budapest. Each door and window had a metal grill on the ground floor level.

A modern-day form of security, but one that would not have helped when the Nazis or the Fascists came knocking.

As we reach the first-floor landing, we troop towards the apartment whose front door was framed by shelves laden with plants and other items to give a more welcoming, homely feel. We receive the heartiest greeting from the current residents, a lawyer and his wife with a three-month-old baby in arms. The fresh whitewashed walls were just as we would have them in modern family life; a home office with a computer on the young lawyer's desk.

I reflect on what might have been the complex set of emotions in that apartment in the 1940s when the family had to leave their home with nothing but the bare necessities they could carry into a place of hiding, not knowing where and for how long. And the time that they closed the front door for the last time with suitcases hastily packed, heading to the other side of the world. Parents with a serious demeanour, a mischievous six-year-old who might have thought they were going on holiday, a mother carrying an infant on her arm who was oblivious of the significance of the occasion.

Having processed the emotions and memories, both real and those long held in our mind's eye, after visiting the apartments, we prepared ourselves for the evening's experience, which I had been told was not to be missed.

The Dohány Street Synagogue

Like many things in Budapest, a visit to the Dohány utca Synagogue, the Grand Synagogue, is unforgettable. The building has many claims to fame, and is the second-largest synagogue in the world. For someone used to the more modestly-sized synagogues of Australia, it is imposing, with the capacity to seat 3,000 people representing the Neolog tradition of liberal-leaning practising Jews— the somewhat progressive modern practising Jewish community.

The location is auspicious. Next door to the synagogue is the residence where the writer and journalist, Tivadar Herzl, (better known internationally as Theodor), who envisioned a Jewish State, was born in 1860. The home has long been demolished but the building now houses the Jewish Museum and is represented by a plaque on both its landing and entrance.

We entered in our best attire, suitably modest for a Sabbath service, and left our iPhones for safe-keeping at the entry point. No photos to be taken during the Sabbath service. We were awe-struck by its size and interior, the magnificent Moorish architecture, the dark timber pews, and the many elements that reflected the historical significance of the building. We attended the Friday evening service, just as my grandfather would have done when taking my older sister for a musical experience.

His was the era pre-radio, television and iPhone, when music was more generally available to be enjoyed in settings outside the home, in churches and in the rare circumstance where a synagogue had an organ, albeit a very famous one that could be enjoyed by community members who were not regular worshippers. My sister, two years older than me, remembers the experience vividly as a special event with our grandfather.

My Budapesti grandfather was an Orthodox Jew who would have attended the orthodox Kazinczy Street Synagogue in Budapest where both my parents and Nándor would have been married in happier days. Nevertheless, he clearly would have enjoyed the organ music that reverberated throughout the Dohány Street Synagogue during the service on this day in 2023. Our guide earlier that day had taken great pains to point out that the Hungarian composer, Franz Liszt, was known to have played there, as had Saint-Saëns in concert performances. Completed in the mid-1800s so there was a wealth of history to reflect upon.

There were famous musicians like Béla Bartók and Franz Lehár. Also Franz Liszt, who had been recognised as a 'superstar' musician around whom 'Lisztomania' developed, somewhat like Beatlemania more than 100 years later. He was a child prodigy who gave his first performance at the age of nine, with a prodigious output giving dynamic performances in 1,000 concerts between 1838 and 1848, known also for his scandalous love affairs.

Liszt was a brilliant virtuoso who must have brought fame and attention to Budapest's glitterati. He was responsible for coining the term 'recital', although his was more than a recital as he played on multiple pianos during the same performance, with each piano facing a different part of the audience. The grandeur of this one space where Liszt would have played to rapt audiences speaks to the way Jewish artists and culture were inextricably woven into the public life of Budapest some 100 years before the Holocaust, and further struggled during the Communist occupation.

On 20th of December 1860, just one year after the dedication of the synagogue, in what was termed the 'Bach era' (the period in Hungarian historiography in which Alexander Bach was the Austrian Minister of the Interior, charged with transforming Hungarian public administration), there were large scale celebrations when the Jewish community of Pest expressed support for the Hungarian nationalist aspirations. (Pest is the historical city that merged with Buda to form Budapest in 1873). Many statesmen, scholars, writers, and artists attended the services regardless of their denominations. This was the first occasion when the crowd, waving national flags, sang the patriotic poem called the 'Proclamation' in the synagogue—behaviour that houses of worship are not known for, but a clear indication of how nationalistic the Hungarian Jewish community of the time felt.

Until the 1940s, Hungarian patriotism and Jewish pride were not at odds with one another. Men like my maternal grandfather were Hungarian ex-World War I Jewish servicemen who wore their badges with pride. There were celebrated Jewish writers, artists, newspaper editors, doctors, lawyers, intellectuals, as well as those active in politics and in rebuilding the economy. Whilst my family was strictly Orthodox, observant in all the practices in a modern way, less than one-third of Hungarian Jews considered themselves Orthodox. They were just part of the ever-changing, but eternally resilient fabric of Hungarian Jewry.

This was an intriguing country, not only for the population of Jews whose practices and loyalty were welcomed, at least in the early years of the 20th century, but for any observer of history. These were times when lands were lost and gained, pride and honour being great features of the country's psyche. Who were these complex people with whom my family history is intrinsically linked, not wanting to be forgotten?

Chapter Three
Who Were the Magyars?

If you want to study war games—profit and loss in territories, friends, neighbours and enemies, Hungary makes a perfect case study. Can we ascribe emotions to a country? A country and a city are collectives comprised of people who lead and those who are led; there is pride for lands gained, and shame and guilt for lands lost. For example, there is a prime minister whose hand is forced to sign a treaty and who then takes his own life, unable to live with the guilt and shame. There are edicts about who can be employed on racial grounds, with whom you can have sex, and who you can marry. These were the mere snippets of what was happening in Hungary in the turbulent years 1940-1945. War, politics and intrigue all feature in the story.

The Hungarian flag is red, white, and green, and there is a ditty in Hungarian *'piros, fehér, zöld, ez a magyar föld'* which translates as 'red, white, and green that is the Hungarian land'. From early years the ditty is sung, enforcing the idea that pride in country and land is what matters—not spiritually, as it is for some indigenous communities that many of us are learning about in the 21st century—but because of its pride-giving and worth.

Hungary is in Central Europe with an area measuring 35,917 square miles (93,025 square kilometres) and an estimated population in 2023 of 9,627,000. In 2023 the capital, Budapest, is a thriving metropolis, proud of its beautiful edifices and repurposing the past. The old Communist era statues and memorabilia are housed in a park, kilometres from central Budapest, waiting to be remembered by those who wish to revisit that moment of history. The much-celebrated 'ruin bars' are nightclubs built around the bombed-out shells of buildings—venues for pleasure by those who are too young to remember the history of death and destruction in World War II

Budapest. But when you track back a little further in time there is a lot to capture one's attention. The people are an amalgam of Magyars and various Slavic, Turkish, and Germanic peoples. The official Hungarian language is Magyar, and the official religion is Christianity (mostly Roman Catholic but also Protestant). Despite Hungary being a member of the European Union, it has retained its own currency, the forint.

Many tales describe the origins of the word 'Hungarian' (*Magyar*), some more embedded in history than others. The one that has childish appeal but may not be historically sound describes how Hungarian and Magyar are derived from a pre-Christian legend about two mythical brothers, *Hunor and Magor*. The legend has it that one day, while hunting deer, the brothers discovered a beautiful land located in the territory of present-day Hungary, where they settled and made their home. Hunor then became the forefather of the *Huns*, while Magor is thought of as the forefather of the *Hungarians*.[1]

Hungary had been considered one of the oldest and largest countries in Europe since the end of the ninth century. It is older than France or Germany. Hungarian territory was first ruled by the Celts, then the Romans. The Hungarians have their unique language, which only a fraction of people around the world can understand, and which is etymologically closest to Finnish and Estonian.

The Hungarians are generally known as proud patriots. They are especially proud of their ancestry, their nation's traditions, culture, and language. Their unshakeable patriotism is also evidenced by the fact that Hungarian children study their homeland and culture as a mandatory subject at school.

Historian and Holocaust survivor Zsuzsanna Ozsváth, author of the 2010 childhood memoir *When the Danube Ran Red*, describes how Hungary was a 'sizable' country in the 12th century until the 15th and 16th centuries, by which time it was occupied by the Turks. There were border issues with some parts belonging to Turkey and some to Hungary, and some to Austria. The Turks stayed for 150 years. In the 13th century, the Tartars killed half the population, so by the 17th century, Hungary was 'almost non-existent'. The Austrians defeated Turkey at the beginning of the 17th century. Hungary at that time had groups of people such as Slovaks, Germans, Croatians, Czechs and Austrians. Austria wanted to rule Hungary, so Hungary became involved in a war with Austria. Finally, in 1848, there was a mass uprising from the Hungarians against the Austrians, and in 1867, there was an agreement between the two countries to become a single country. The Austro-Hungarian monarchy became, in national terms, a 'fast-developing monarchy'. It was proudly known to its many patriots as the Austro-Hungarian Empire.

Ozsváth describes Nationalism as being 'when millions of people believe that they have been wrongly done by' which may be a good explanation for the nationalistic pride evident in Hungary. So, when World War I resulted in the signing of the Treaty of Trianon[2] on 4 June 1920 at the Grand Trianon Palace in Versailles and the subsequent dissolution of the Austro-Hungarian Empire, Hungary lost two-thirds of its territory and much of its pride. The various groups of Czechs, Slovaks, Poles, Serbs and Croatians moved in and there was a corresponding rise in nationalism; with that, a growing need for scapegoats to justify their losses and save their self-respect.

Miklós Horthy was a general who headed one part of Hungary's military. During the period of civil violence known as the 'white terror' that followed the collapse of the Austro-Hungarian empire, his men shot about 2,000 people between winter 1919 and spring 1920, when Horthy became Regent[3] and leader of Hungary. According to Ozsváth, in a specific burst of targeted antisemitism, Horthy went out with troops which he called 'my police' in 1919 and 1920, shooting Jews arbitrarily into the Danube and into the Tisza on the pretext that they were communists. Then came the Depression, and the consideration was how close Hungary should be to Germany; Horthy decided 'as close as possible'.

Hungary had had a chequered history in the interwar period and there were many losses of troops and men. But somehow Budapest seems to have recovered each time and rose like a Goddess to be lauded and promoted in cinemas.

In 1938 when there was a great deal of tension and terror in Europe, Metro Goldwyn-Mayer presented James A. Fitzpatrick's travel talks: 'The Voice of the Globe'. I watch this film clip that attempts to draw the tourists into Budapest, much as they are being drawn in today.

The film clip narration begins:

> *Bracing the banks of the Danube River is the beautiful city of Budapest which was formally a combination of two cities Buda on the left and Pest on Right—during the last 50 years it has increased from 300,000 persons to one million and houses one of the biggest Parliament buildings in the world. A country which has lived through an interesting history and was formally an important part of the great Austro-Hungarian Empire which had disintegrated by the last War. The shopping districts are on a par with the best of those of modern cities. It had not suffered traffic congestion. In 1849 the chain bridge was completed, the first of its kind in Europe. At first it was thought that there wasn't sufficient clearance for large steam ships, but in an ingenious way the smokestacks lean backwards as the steam ships pass under the bridge. Impressively situated on a hill is the Royal Palace. During the reign of Queen Maria Theresa—Saint Stephen' (István) Coronation Church, named in honour of the first king of Hungary who was reportedly crowned by the Pope as the first Christian king of Hungary, and by this act Hungary became separated from the east and brought into the fold of Western civilisation. On an island stands the Museum of Hungarian Agriculture, considered to be one of the best constructed buildings of Europe. Budapest is noted for its colourful outdoor restaurants. Hospitality atmospheres are a mix of the music of Ferenc Liszt and glorified gypsy music. On Margaret's Island there is a thermal grotto where it is said that once a holy man lived and*

> brought miraculous cures by bathing people in the thermal springs. One of the of the largest swimming pools on Margaret's Island is kept in-tact by artificial walls, and five million gallons of water flow from the variegated springs every day. There are about 80 outdoor swimming pools—one of the most popular is St Gellert's, where artificial waves are created by a mechanical device at the far end of the pool.

That famous river has inspired one of the world's immortal waltzes. And the beautiful visual images continue as the film ends with the waltz—'The Blue Danube' by Johann Strauss.

The idyllic film seems particularly innocent, almost Pollyanna-ish, considering the years that were to follow. When the film first rolled out in cinemas, designed to entice monied foreign tourists to visit, Hungary was already entrenching the antisemitism that had found new purchase in the country's nationalism and law.

Already in the middle of the 1930s, the Jews of Hungary were increasingly anxious; as the historian Ozsváth describes, there was a constant 'clamouring voice' in the media and in politics against the Jews.

In neighbouring Germany, Hitler took the reins of power in 1933, and so began the start of his rigorous anti-Jewish campaign. By 1935 there were comprehensive anti-Jewish laws in Germany which were heavy and threatening at both national and state levels, essentially restricting Jews in all aspects of public and private life and segregating them from the Aryan population. Other central and Eastern European powers with their own anti-Semitic bent were paying close attention.

In Hungary at this time, the laws were more about restricting the numbers of Jewish personnel in professions and leadership, not yet outright persecution; rather there was a resentment of the Jewish trend of success. Already in the 1920s there was a law known as Article XXV, also known as the *Numerous Clausus,* which placed a 5 per cent limit on university admissions of Jews.

In 1937 when Miklós Horthy's reactionary forces came into power in Hungary, what followed was a brutal repression of Hungarian Jewry and a series of anti-Jewish policies which intensified in 1938 and continued into the war years. In March 1939, the Hungarian Labor Force Service System, drafting Jewish men from the ages of 18 to 48 into forced labour units, was established.

Pál Teleki took over as Hungarian Prime Minister on 15 February 1939, as the previous Prime Minister, Hungarian Prime Minister Béla Imrédy, was found to have been unacceptably of Jewish descent. Teleki joined the Tripartite Pact (better known as the Berlin Pact) to join Germany, Italy and Japan as the fourth power in the Axis alliance. Despite joining the alliance, he had wanted to keep Hungary neutral in the early stages of the war. He was in office until April 3, 1941, when he took his own life with a pistol that evening, having felt betrayed when the German troops marched through Hungary on their way to invading Yugoslavia, effectively ending Hungarian neutrality.

In addition to the political shenanigans with Germany and the allies, there were internal ructions with the feeling that Jews were overrepresented in public life. Between 1938 and 1944, 21 discriminatory laws were passed. There were three main ones called the 'Jewish Laws', more accurately, the *anti-*Jewish laws.

Although the earlier law was passed in 1920, what became known as the First Jewish Law (or the First anti-Jewish Law) was passed in May 1938. For example, Article no. V 1938 limited the number of Jewish people who could practise law, journalism, or be a physician, and there were to be no more than 20 per cent Jews in financial and commercial theatre, film, and the press and in businesses employing more than 10 people.

Article no. IV 1939 (known as the Second Jewish Law or anti-Jewish Law) brought more restrictions, which, for example, said that Jews could not teach in any school other than a Jewish one; nor work as a doctor in certain hospitals; couldn't be a judge, nor attend Universities. The law defined who was considered a Jew, taking the German definitions. An individual qualified as racially Jewish—even if they were baptised as Christian—if more than two grandparents were Jewish and even if their grandparents were baptised as Christian. Article no. XV (known as the Third Jewish Law or anti-Jewish Law) of 1941, based on racist ideology, prohibited marriage and intercourse between Christian and Jew.

All these freedom-limiting restrictions seem to have been tolerated. Likely that there was no recourse or easy alternative. Most people, like my family, were not ready to take the escape route to some far-flung place, although some did, without language nor possessions. How much repression would we accept today, having enjoyed so many years of freedom, intellectual and personal? It is this undercurrent that rises to surface these questions when reading this history.

Meanwhile Hungary became increasingly more closely aligned with Hitler. Horthy watched closely. He had the hope and expectation that through German influence Hungary would regain the lands that had been taken away. Hitler gave Hungary a chunk of Magyar-speaking Slovakia. Shortly thereafter, Hungary enacted a stronger version of the lapsed First anti-Jewish Law of 1920.

On 27 September 1940, Hitler signed the Tri-Power Pact with Italy and Japan. Hungary joined the pact on 2 November, and Hungary formally became an ally of Germany. In July and August 1941, the Hungarian government ordered the roundup and deportation of 'Jewish foreign nationals'—those not holding Hungarian citizenship.

Twenty-two thousand Hungarian gendarmerie, a rural paramilitary police force with the assistance of local police officers in towns and cities, were tasked to deport the foreign Jews. That is, the refugees who had fled from other parts of Europe to Hungary as well as many born elsewhere. The Police Force was initially a civilian organisation, although during World War II it became increasingly paramilitary in character, and received its orders from the Budapest Chief of Police and the national Chief of Police, who exercised authority over all police forces outside of the capital. Thus, the corralling of large sections of the population was executed efficiently in the 1940s.

Approximately 18,000 Jews were sent to the Ukrainian city of Kamenets-Podolsky where they were murdered by SS killing units in mass executions starting from 27 August 1941. The recorded words of the survivors of the massacres reveal the horrors of the time, including witnessing distressing mutilations, people being buried alive, and parents being machine-gunned down in front of their children. The 'cleansing' also involved deporting Jews across the Soviet and Romanian border.

In 1942-44 approximately 42,000 labour-service Jews were taken to the Soviet front where the temperatures for five months are minus 40 degrees, so most froze to death. Out of the Jewish forced labourers, a mere 1,000 survived. The rest froze to death or died when they were made to clear minefields left behind by Russian armed forces.

Hitler's presence reached Hungary on 15 March 1944, demanding deportations. The tyrant was already worried about the future of his genocidal quest. The tide was turning against the Germans in the war, and the Nazis were concerned that the Hungarians might broker a separate peace deal with the Allies which would jeopardise completion of their 'Final Solution to the Jewish Question'.

On 18 March 1944, Hitler summoned Regent Horthy to the Schloss Klesheim in Austria to inform him that the Hungarians would continue as Germany's allies and 'Operation Margarette', the occupation of Hungary and the extermination of Hungarian Jewry would begin immediately with Adolf Eichmann, Dieter Wisliceny and Hermann A. Krumey in charge.

Eichmann arrived in Budapest with a relatively small cohort of 150-200 SS personnel on 19 March and the occupation of Hungary officially began on 21 March. To achieve what he did in a short period of time the Hungarians would have had to help him. He himself was only in Budapest for six months, a short time in which to round up and dispose of 600,000 Jews.

The first transport of Hungarian Jewry arrived in the notorious extermination concentration camp of Auschwitz on 2 May 1944, and a massive deportation campaign began on 15 May.

More recently, I was gifted a loan of a rare treasure, Eugene (Jenö) Lévai's *Black Book on the Martyrdom of Hungarian Jewry*, edited and translated into English, published in 1948. The author was commissioned by the Hungarian Government to write a comprehensive report of wartime events soon after war's end, when there was cooperation and access to records. The volume is replete with verbatim records of meetings, newspaper reports and cabinet papers. For example:

> 'After the constitution of the Jewish Council, the only official Jewish organ permitted to operate in the city, the *Newspaper of the Hungarian Jews*, published the first instructions to be issued by the Germans:
>
> *... On definitive instructions received from the competent authorities, we herewith announce the principles to be observed and the line of action to be followed and obligatory to everyone concerned. Everyone must remain at his post, must continue to do his duty and must devote his full energy to the work required of him by the authorities. We wish it to be known, on the basis of a definite statement to this effect issued by the competent authorities, that the commercial, cultural and social existence of the Jews is to continue undisturbed. The announcement will reassure everyone. The wish has been expressed for a Jewish Council to be formed in order to represent the Jews. This Council will have the right to appoint sub-committees for the purpose of attending to detail work. The Central Jewish Council is the only authorised and responsible body representing the whole of Hungarian Jewry and it is the body authorised to maintain contact with the German authorities.*

> *It has been stated that no one will be arrested because of his Jewish origin. Should arrests prove necessary, these will be due entirely different reasons ...*[4]

Numerous reasons were detailed, such as leaving Budapest, or country people coming to Budapest, or for breaking any of the countless laws that had been passed. The tenor of the statement, or more accurately an edict, is almost a hypnotic way of lulling people into complacency that they would be OK if they didn't break ever increasingly harsh laws.

When the story of Eichmann's arrival was recorded in Lévai's *Black Book* and there were 'concerns within the Jewish community' the official Government circles were labelling these inquiries as 'Jewish rumours and scares'. One man, János Gábor was instructed to question Eichmann. 'His answer was: "If the Hungarian Jews behave themselves and do not join the Ruthenian partisans, there will be no deportations." Eichmann made this statement at the end of May. And the "wise" Jews of Budapest believed him!'[5]

By 8 July, more than 437,000 Hungarian Jews had been sent to Auschwitz, and 90 per cent went directly from the trains to the gas chambers. Most of the Jews who perished came from the Hungarian countryside, as did my aunt Mati from Makó. Despite final-hour attempts at eradication, 100,000 Jews in Budapest did manage to survive. Clearly, we were the fortunate ones.

But a lot was happening for that 100,000 to make survival possible. Good people were hard at work.

But as I read the recorded statements and decrees, they raise questions about civil obedience, when to believe and when to doubt? When to challenge, and when to resist or run, if escape routes were to be found? And when you are trapped without an escape route, when do you do as you are told? If you are part of the leadership, as Nándor must have been, do you accept orders and instructions and do as best as you can under the circumstances? In the mayhem of ghettos, hidden by strangers, avoiding bombs and destruction, there were those 100,000 who somehow survived.

The Ghetto of Budapest

In the final seven weeks of the war, precisely on 18 November 1944, the government informed the Jewish Council that the Ghetto of Budapest was to be set up for those Jews who were still there. Ghettoisation throughout Hungary, starting in the regions, began earlier that year on 7 April. By 16 April, a full directive was signed by László Baky, a leading member of the Hungarian far-right Arrow Cross movement who held various positions in the government.

The Royal Hungarian Government would cleanse the country of Jews within a short time. Baky gave the directive.

SUBJECT: *The Assignment of Dwelling Places for Jews*

> *The Royal Hungarian Government will soon have the country purged of Jews. I order the purge to be carried out by regions. As a result of the purge, Jewry—irrespective of sex or age—is to be transported to assigned concentration camps. In towns or large villages a part of the Jews are later to be accommodated in Jewish buildings or ghettos, assigned to them by the police authorities.*[6]

The decree went on for several pages and was brought into effect, first in the regions and then in Budapest. The regions outside Budapest were brutally cleansed of their Jewish populations in a matter of months. Meanwhile the ghettoisation of Budapest came into effect some seven months later.

In Budapest, 63,000 Jews were to be transferred to an average room density of 14 Jews per room. The ghetto had an area of 0.3 kilometres (0.1 miles), a small fraction of the city's 207 square kilometres (80 square miles). Jewish citizens had to report property with estimated values to the State Financial Directorate, special attention to be paid to art, carpets, silver etc. Jews could only withdraw 1,000 pengős (the Hungarian currency from 1927-1946) per month, barely a subsistence level of cash.

The Jewish population of Budapest was to vacate 6,000 apartments outside the ghetto area to provide apartments for the Christians affected by the relocations. They were to gather at Klauzál Tér and take only what they could carry. Dohány Street was the boundary. The movement of people began towards the end of November and was completed by December 2. Many were attacked, robbed, and murdered on the way to the ghetto by the Nyilas, otherwise known as the Arrow Cross, the Hungarian fascists whose reign of terror was most prominent towards the end of 1944. The ghetto was officially sealed on 10 December, with four gates, each guarded by the Nyilas cadres and policemen.

My imaginings run riot; although there is some evidence that children can recall events in the first two years of their lives, for me it is not my memory as a 15-month-old, but rather the facts as they are printed on the pages by recorders of history, the memories of those who have given testimony, and the photographic images that are available for me to stare at. The figures and numbers in the texts signify very little without the human faces that give meaning to the statistics.

People were rushing about, some taking bare necessities in the expectation that their stay would not be too long, others taking their most valuable possessions, perhaps already sewn into the linings of their overcoats—after all, a piece of jewellery could buy some life-saving favour or food from an unexpected quarter. The rushing around would be during the daytime, as there were curfews already in place at night. And those who straggled would be subjected to attacks by the Nyilas.

And then there are the images of thousands of people six deep against the ghetto's wooden wall, moving in an orderly fashion whilst gendarmes stand guard. But where is there to run? The crowd of thousands move like lambs on their way to slaughter. The big difference is that these are human beings carrying baskets or bundles of clothing or bedding hoisted over one shoulder, or in a roll against their back. They wear a yellow star on their winter coats, and their bowed heads appear ghost-like with disbelief that it has come to this in beautiful Budapest.

There is one haunting image of those who are marching towards somewhere within the wall of the ghetto. A man on stilts wearing a black cape displaying the yellow star, dressed like the Grim Reaper, his face covered with a white mask stands close to the guard, reminding those entering that this roundup is indeed grim, so beware. Once inside the gate there is no going out. In fact, for the first six days you could only be in the streets for two hours a day between 9.00 am and 11.00 am. Except if you were working for the Jewish Council or the embassy of a neutral country, like my uncle Nándor seems to have done. Indeed, on one official document he listed his title as 'Embassy Official' but did not name the embassy.

Infants would be oblivious to the changes. Crowding might even keep them closer to their parents, but children who were a little older would pick up on the distress and anxiety that the adults were experiencing. After all, there is the lived phenomenon of second-hand stress. And those tensions and stresses would possibly manifest as post-traumatic stress disorder many years later.

Whilst the first few weeks were sombre and orderly, people settled as they do when disasters like floods or bushfires strike and people are thrust together. But the mood would have changed as they heard banging on the doors, saw marauding gangs or observed shootings and massacres within the walls. The Nyilas penetrated virtually every building, reigning fear and dread upon the inhabitants. They also went to great lengths to round up people who were in hiding outside the walls, so people continued to pour into the ghetto.

By January 1945 the ghetto population reached 70,000. Most of them were children under 16, the ill, and men and women over 50. The increase was due to the large number of protected Jews from the International ghetto which had been set up after 23 October in the Pozsonyi Street neighbourhood. The population consisted of Swiss, Swedish, Spanish, Portuguese and Vatican missions, and 6,000 children who had been placed in the care of the Red Cross by their parents, much as I had been.

Carl Lutz and Raoul Wallenberg, representing the Swiss and Swedish ambassadors respectively, protested, but that 'note' of protest reached the relevant authorities too late, after the children had already been transferred into the ghetto. The decision-makers were not going to reverse that. The influx was also due to those Jews who were in hiding but were dragged into the ghetto by the Nyilas.

I read and reread the description of the ghetto, as the thought of such a lock-up and imprisonment of humans is hard to imagine. Some witness testimonies describe these conditions 40-60 years after the experience. So official records are helpful in aiding our understanding, as memories may be somewhat deceptive in both under- and over-dramatizing the experience.

Although the ghetto existed for only seven weeks, there was a well-developed administrative apparatus for the area which was divided into 10 districts with allocated leaders and deputy leaders.

Within the ghetto, police maintained law and order, although little was required until later, when the ghetto was invaded by the Nyilas. Uniformed and non-uniformed personnel looted and murdered large numbers of residents, which finally resulted in only two gates in and out of the ghetto being in operation for the purpose of control.

There was hunger. The food allocation was 690-790 calories (prison inmates received 1500). By 25 December, when Budapest was encircled by the Russian forces, the food became scarcer, and cases of starvation increased. In addition to hunger, overcrowding, lack of water and the piling of rubbish, meant that health and hospital conditions became desperate. Meanwhile, the corpses piled up.

According to the historian Braham, the scenes at the makeshift hospitals evoked images of Dante's inferno'.⁷

They had to cope with the increasing number of dead bodies, including the hundreds of suicides.

There were plans for the Germans to mass murder the inhabitants of the ghetto before retreating, but the advance of the Soviet forces led to their liberation in April 1945.

Earlier in September 1944, the Russian army continued marching west and crossed the Hungarian border. Horthy tried to negotiate peace with the Soviets and, in October, ordered the Hungarian troops to surrender. But Nazi Germany orchestrated a coup to overthrow the Regent Horthy. On 15 October, the Hungarian far-right ultra nationalist Ferenc Szálasi, the ex-military man and now head of the Arrow Cross Party, led the coup. Subsequently, Szálasi became prime minister and head of state. Then came the reign of terror that ended up on the banks of the Danube and in the streets of Budapest. In a grim echo of the antisemitic massacres a quarter-century earlier, Jews were paraded naked through the streets, marched to the banks of the river, lined up, and gunned down, for their dead and dying bodies to be swept downstream. The Danube ran red with the blood of the victims.⁸

After the German occupation in 1944, the war arrived in the city in earnest with the Siege of Budapest, starting in September when the Soviets surrounded the capital. Eighty per cent of the buildings of Budapest were destroyed or damaged, including all the bridges, as well as the Parliament Building and Buda Castle. The Chain Bridge had collapsed into the Danube, as if weeping for what was lost.

During the siege of Budapest, the ghetto was hit by artillery 27 times. Initially, ways were found to bury the dead, as is necessary in the Jewish tradition, soon after death, although after 3 January, the bodies could not be removed from the ghetto. Some were stored in the tubs of the ritual bath houses in Kazinczy Street, some piled up 'like lumber' in commercial establishments in Klauzál Tér, and others in the courtyard of the Dohány Synagogue. When the ghetto was liberated on 17 January 1945 there were approximately 3,000 bodies awaiting burial. Eventually 2,218 bodies were buried in mass graves, in the garden surrounding the Heroes Temple, adjacent to the Dohány Street Synagogue.

The number of Jews who died in Budapest in 1944-1945 was close to 17,000.

Today, the garden is known as the graveyard of martyrs. Many bodies were reclaimed by families and reburied, while some 2,000 bodies remain in mass graves, many beneath the courtyard of the synagogue which now houses the Raoul Wallenberg Holocaust Memorial Park.

I was introduced to the courtyard early on the day we had visited Dohány Street Synagogue. We saw the weeping willow, heavily laden with leaves that would droop with sorrow and tears, if a metallic sculpture were able to weep. I could have stood there all day looking for the names of relatives—names I had only just heard about—an uncle who had lost a wife and nine children, and too many relatives of family friends, along with the 'modest' recognition of Kasztner and the plaque to Wallenberg and Lutz.

The garden is a reminder of the ravaged, beautiful city in which my siblings and I were born, and only narrowly managed to escape. It is these years that my family only survived through the heroism of Nándor, along with the help of the Budapesti Schindlers and their embassies.

Chapter Four
Nándor

My mother's brother, Ferdinánd (Fred as he was known to some in Australia), or Nándor Eichel, was a key figure in my family. Mystery and silence have shrouded his wartime activities. My ongoing suspicion that he played a major role in protecting our family, and that he was actively involved in the rescue efforts, both overt and covert, to save the lives of many Hungarian Jews, propelled my early research.

One of my fondest childhood memories is receiving the gift of a banana from my 'Uncle Nándi', as he was affectionately known to many, including us. It is a very particular feature of Hungarian names that they frequently have an affectionate derivative or diminutive. For example, in my family I was always addressed as 'Eri'.

But I digress. I can still remember the sweet taste of that banana. I originally decided to give my memoir the nostalgic title, *Taste of a Banana* to honour my uncle's memory. The family memoir has been written, but often the personal and relational detail in such writings is sanitised to respect those who have passed or who are still alive; and written from the perspective of a childhood experience.

Now wanting to more broadly address the plight of Hungarian Jews during World War II, and my personal fascination with the role played by my uncle during those tumultuous years, I have been inspired to undertake more extensive research that would underpin my understanding as an adult.

We always thought warmly of Uncle Nándi—and considered him an important person in our lives. He helped save me in my first year of life; he was the first to greet us after we left Budapest, to gift me with that banana; and he was my mother's constant source of support in Australia.

I learn that Nándi had amazing power and influence! He was well connected in Budapest, and he remained my parents' best friend in Australia, as well as our medical, financial and family matters advisor.

However, there was always both a mystery and a modesty about Nándi. He was something of an enigma as he displayed a general unwillingness to talk about himself and the past. When I became interested in the Holocaust and family history, I made a trip to Sydney in 1996, tape recorder in hand, in an attempt to record his story, and through that to capture our family history. I knew that he had refused to give testimony to the Spielberg archives[1] which had been established for the explicit purpose of capturing Holocaust survivors' testimony in their own words. Nándi, who was 86 at the time, used the occasion of my visit to deflect the conversation from my purpose in every possible way. He asked questions about me and my family, and the hours rolled on. Alas, I had a plane to catch so left without having turned on my tape recorder. It was clear that no amount of conversation would lead him to give details of his wartime experiences for the record.

Given his active part in the war and his unwillingness to talk about it, my imagination ran wild, especially when I came to know Rezső Kasztner's story and realised that their lives must have intersected in some way.

Rezső Kasztner was born in 1906 in Kolozsvár, which at the time was part of the Kingdom of Hungary. The city did not become part of Romania until 1920, following the Treaty of Trianon. Later, during the Second Vienna Award in 1940, parts of Transylvania, including Kolozsvár were returned to Hungary. Kasztner was a lawyer and a journalist and has been described as a Jewish intellectual, an analytical and strategic thinker. In Kolozsvár he was a journalist for *Új Kelet, (New East)* a Hungarian language newspaper with Zionist leanings, and also as a lawyer assistant for Dr József Fischer, a lawyer and member of Parliament and president of the Jewish Community of Kolozsvár. When the Germans closed the newspaper, Kasztner moved to Budapest in 1941 where he worked in the aid and rescue of Jews, particularly those who were fleeing countries occupied by the Germans.

From the summer of 1944 until the collapse of the Third Reich, Kasztner played a dangerous game with Adolf Eichmann. Kasztner's stated goal was to do deals—trading gold, diamonds, and cash—to arrange trains to transport Jews out of Hungary. As a consequence of extensive negotiations, Eichmann sent Joel Brand, a representative of the international Jewish Welfare Organisation known as the Joint Distribution Committee (JDC), and Bandi Grosz, a Hungarian Jew who had worked for Hungarian and German military intelligence, rather than Kasztner, to Istanbul to do a deal with the Allies. The deal involved releasing Hungarian Jews from Hungary in exchange for trucks and impossible sums of money. That meant Kasztner was forced to stay behind to deal with Eichmann.

Ultimately, Kasztner and others from the JDC successfully organised for 35 cattle trucks to leave Budapest on 30 June 1944 with 1,684 Jewish passengers, including 273 children. The 150 wealthiest passengers purportedly paid the equivalent of $1000 per person, in currency, gold, jewels and shares of stock collected by the Jewish committee. The journey took several weeks, with a diversion to Bergen-Belsen concentration camp, before the trucks finally reached Switzerland between August and December. Passengers included members of Kasztner's family and 388 Jews from the ghetto in Kolozsvár, Kasztner's birthplace.

After the war, Kasztner settled in Israel, where postwar tensions were high. There were battles to fight with the surrounding hostile nations; political struggles to deal with in establishing a government; and in the midst of economic hardships, refugees to absorb. Israelis saw themselves as the 'New Jews'—handsome and swarthy—builders of a nation, tillers of the soil—wanting to distance themselves from the old. Israel replaced Yiddish with Hebrew language as the country wanted to normalise. The Hungarian survivors felt that Israelis didn't understand their plight or the depths of their suffering.

In that climate, the behaviour of turning away and not wanting to listen was also a global phenomenon reverberating wherever survivors went, in Israel and beyond. There was not much time or sympathy for the Hungarian survivors.

Kasztner was later branded a Nazi collaborator. He was accused of selecting his own friends and family to travel on the transport out of Budapest, while abandoning the Jews who were left behind. He was also accused of not warning the Hungarian Jews of the fate that awaited them on the trains bound for Auschwitz. All part of the controversy that continues to plague Kasztner beyond the grave.

After migrating to Israel in 1947 and leading a high-profile life as a spokesperson for the Ministry of Trade and Industry, Kasztner was involved in a protracted trial where he was accused of using his relationship with Eichmann, which included drinking spirits and smoking cigars together, to further his own ends. Perhaps he was just drinking and smoking as a way of keeping the bartering alive.

This was the circle in Budapest that my uncle must have moved in, aware of the trading and attempts to rescue Jews with bribery, both overt and covert. But my supposition is that the lesson for him was that it was better to remain silent, a non-entity, or at least not draw attention to yourself; just get on with your work, rather than be conspicuous; have others ask: What did you do during the war? Perhaps be in danger of being branded a traitor, as a decision to save a few important rabbis could leave you failing many others. These are the insights that Nándor would have considered when choosing to stay silent, rather than imprint the public record.

I reflect on the countless ethical dilemmas that individuals in the heat of war would have been confronted with, such as who to save and who to leave behind, along with moment-by-moment decisions that might have massive consequences. How harshly or how kindly we judge our own decisions post-event is complicated by how we think others might judge our actions years later, in a different political and social climate. The mere thought can leave one traumatised. 'Best not to disclose and discuss' could be a personal mantra that many adopted at war's end.

In Anna Porter's detailed historical book about Kasztner, there was no mention of Nándor Eichel. For many years, I searched high and low to trace a connection between the two men. I searched the recorded sources of the war years in Budapest at Yad Vashem, the Holocaust Remembrance Centre in Jerusalem, the Washington Holocaust Museum, and the Memorial Museum of Hungarian Speaking Jewry in Safed, Israel.

The Memorial Museum of Hungarian Speaking Jewry

On 27 July 2023 we visit the Memorial Museum of Hungarian Speaking Jewry in Safed, Israel, where my first online attempts at research had not been successful. On the hottest July day on record, we drove from Tel Aviv to Safed and were greeted by a unique sight in a hilly enclave, the home for a community of artists in the highest city in Israel, with a history dating back to the Crusaders. The museum building is located in the grounds of what was once Government House, built by the Turkish Government in 1889. With the liberation of Safed in 1948, the main building was used as a military recruiting base and the first swearing-in of Israeli soldiers took place there. The place is both a house with a history and one that houses history.

The Museum's Director is Ron Lustig whose late father, Yosef, started the museum with his wife Hava after settling in Israel and retiring to the locality. Yosef and Hava wanted the museum to tell the story of a complex, vibrant world with rich cultures and transformations that culminated in the terrible period of Hungary's Holocaust experience. Thirty-seven years later, the museum is housed in that Ottoman-era stone building with an amazing extensive library—a collection of documents, memorabilia and artifacts that tell the story of the period and to which are added some harrowing individual family experiences.

The library is the pulsing heart of the museum where the founder, Hava, at the age of 93, has ways of readily accessing information. When I mentioned that my father's family had come from a town in Hungary called Makó, within minutes she had her hands on several volumes relating to that town. We discussed its surrounds, with onion and garlic as the major agricultural commodities; Hava seemed very knowledgeable; I could have stayed talking to her for hours, but there was business to get down to.

Having reached a dead end in my search for Nándor Eichel, a search I first started in 2014, I was keen to learn more about Rezső Kasztner. We sit down with Ron Lustig and engage in conversation about the museum and my interest in seeing copies of *Új Kelet*, a Hungarian-language newspaper that brought news of international events of interest to Jewish Hungarian readers. The paper featured as part of my childhood although I had not learned to read Hungarian. It did not seem important to our parents that we do so. *Új Kelet* was the only newspaper I recall seeing in our home during my childhood. I was highly curious as to how the Kasztner story had been reported in that publication.

I try to show how much I have learned from Porter's book and share my understanding of the Kasztner story. I had finished her book for the second time on the flight to Tel Aviv as I attempted to absorb the micro-detail of his story.

Ron calls his assistant who brings four dossiers—we look at relevant pages of *Új Kelet*—it is all there, except for the very issue I was keen to get hold of with the announcement of and reaction to Kasztner's early death in Israel, the culmination of events set in motion years earlier, in occupied Budapest. At least Porter has described that event, even describing Kasztner's encounter with his killers outside the apartment on that fateful night. Additionally, I had seen film footage of the reenactment of those events.

Ron Lustig wanted to correct some of the common misconceptions about Kasztner and the interventions that had been attributed to him. He considers that, for example, there were four transports, two from Szeged and two from Debrecen which left Hungary. The Szeged transports contained some members of my family, the Strauszes from Makó— the train was scheduled for Auschwitz, but the Mayor of Vienna had asked for extra workers, so the trains were diverted to Strasshof, which was considered to be a 'soft concentration camp' in Austria.

Those who were on these trains that were diverted to Strasshof in June 1944 rather than complete the horrendous journey to Auschwitz were fortunate. Ron did not think that it was due to Kasztner's intervention that the trains were diverted from Auschwitz to Strasshof, a momentous achievement.[2]

However, there was nothing 'soft' about these experiences that ended in survival for the lucky few. I later read the detailed recording of events by the historian Randolph Braham[3] of the roundups, collections, and ghettoisation; each was a horrendous experience.

•••

The Museum has many clippings from *Új Kelet* and the Kasztner trial. These were amongst the reasons that I'd travelled here, searching for a key link missing from the story of the Budapesti Schindlers. Much to my disappointment, when we checked the archive, we found that the editions that announced the outcome of Kasztner's sensational trial and the dramatic aftermath were missing. Ron thinks that the previous borrower, from a reputable university in Tel Aviv, must have also been preoccupied with the major events that rocked Israel's political and judicial system in the 1950s. The researcher seemed to have removed the relevant clippings from the folder. But there is plenty of evidence that *Új Kelet* carried the story of the Kasztner trial as it progressed.

After much conversing, we view a mandatory video that depicts the history of the Museum, and then we are taken on a brief tour. The Museum is replete with memorable objects, some of which are graphically disturbing given the reality that is recorded there. For example, the yellow star with no signifier, because the edict to wear the yellow star came from one day to the next, so there was no time to make them commercially or to *embroider* them in some way; they are just a home-spun item that was compulsory to wear from 5 April 1944. There is a girl's golden hair braid left behind for safekeeping, and found by the father who had survived, only to return to Budapest to find the empty apartment with neither wife nor child. He found his daughter's braid that had been cut before the family were forced to leave the apartment. He also collected his daughter's dress. The father kept both items with him for the rest of his life.

There were images and related displays of those who had saved others, amongst them Carl Lutz, Raoul Wallenberg and Rezső Kasztner. Kasztner's daughter, now a mature woman, came to a significant event at the Museum. She reportedly 'fled in tears' when she saw her father was represented less significantly as a hero than how she saw him. He was placed amongst the many heroes who were active in 1940s Hungary, including an impressive bust of Wallenberg.

Several weeks later, after my return to Melbourne, I received some good news. My request for information about Nándor arrived in the Inbox on my computer. The researchers at the Museum had located a footnote about him in Randolph L. Braham's book *A Népirtás Politikája* p. 1103, note no. 32. The book is called in English: *The Politics of Genocide: The Holocaust in Hungary (1981)*.

The footnote in the two-volume Hungarian-language authoritative text on the period reads:

> *Note 32: Among the MIPI Officials of the Magyar Probation Office (Welfare Bureau of Hungarian Jews, Magyar Izraeliták Pártfogó Irodája) MIPI was ... Nándor Eichel ... stood out in their work, then references the source: Szürke könyv, magyar zsidók megmentéséről, the Gray Book on the Rescue of Hungarian Jews by Lévai Jenö.*[3]

The note in the Gray Book, (which to date has not been translated into English but which with the help of Google Translate), reads:

> *We should also mention the members of the Probation Office dedicated staff. For example ...Nándor Eichel visited the prisoners of Tolonchaz (detention centre) on a regular basis. They have done amazing things by saving lives. Hundreds of people have been removed from departing transports with false papers by becoming 'Aryans' with fake pars... (official documents)*

The text of the actual email was clearly a translation and provided some clarification that men who had been placed in detention, probably in an internment camp awaiting deportation, were saved by receiving identity papers, genuine or false, that allowed them to be freed.

This was the work that Nándor was involved in, with an organization known as MIPI, which was set up in 1938 by the Neolog, Orthodox and Status Quo communities, the first two being the two large communal organisations among Hungarian Jewry. These three were joined in 1939 by the Zionists, and the organisation was known as the Welfare Bureau of Hungarian Jewry.

It's a rare glimpse into a history he seemed determined would not be recorded in any capacity—official or otherwise. In the Museum, as elsewhere, Nándor proved elusive.

Grandchildren as historians

Nándor agreed to go on the record in one source, albeit for a school project. It is a beautiful piece of writing by his eldest granddaughter, Devorah. I had the benefit of drawing on that written history. Whilst much of it was quite detailed, as a teenage researcher draws on her grandfather's story, it shed a little more light on my maternal family, but disappointingly little on Nándor's exploits during the war.

Nándor continued to practise medicine in Bondi Junction, Sydney until a few months before his death on 12 April 1998. Two decades later, Nándor's youngest granddaughter, Tamara, an anaesthetist, published an article in the history supplement of *Anaesthesia and Intensive Care*, 2017, about Nándor's inaugural dissertation on the impact of polio in the 1940s and how it was managed at The University Children's Hospital, Zurich. The original dissertation, written in German in 1951 as part of Nándor's medical studies, was found in his son Robert's home.

Within her article, Tamara recounted a communication with a fellow doctor regarding a patient's care. During the professional discourse, he asked if she was related to a general practitioner, Dr Eichel from Mackenzie St in Bondi Junction. She explained that he was her grandfather.

'Well, he saved my mother's life,' he said. Our conversation had now shifted from professional to personal. He told me that Dr Eichel had secured papers for his mother during World War II in Hungary which helped her to survive the war.

'If it wasn't for him,' he said, 'we wouldn't be having this conversation.'

Clearly, my uncle was an important figure during those wartime years, assisting people in numerous ways to survive. Additionally, in my family, as I have mentioned, he was a significant figure throughout our wartime struggles and subsequent survival, facilitating our departure from Hungary and subsequently providing support, both tangible and emotional, throughout my family's life in Sydney.

Furthermore, he was a hero to many, some yet to be identified. My family was amongst the fortunate few who survived the war and were able to exit Hungary safely and thrive in Australia, Argentina, the US, and Israel. Since my extended family has, in the main, remained observant Jews, there has been a blossoming of family life with dozens of descendants enjoying freedom and good fortune. My uncle Nándor has much to be proud of, and we have a lot to be thankful for.

⋯

My mother had three siblings: two brothers and a sister called Rose (Rózsi) who was born in 1916. Her oldest brother Max (Misi), born in 1910, was tall and curly-haired, with skin so dark that to me he looked African, or perhaps Turkish. There is a lot in the history of Hungary that might explain those tall, swarthy looks which today could be affirmed by DNA testing.

Her younger brother, Ferdinánd (Nándor) Nachman, was born in Budapest on 30 August 1914, soon after Archduke Franz Ferdinand's murder in Sarajevo by Gavrilo Princip that plunged the Austro-Hungarian Empire into war. Due to that momentous event, Nándor was named after the Archduke, as well as his maternal grandfather, because according to Jewish tradition, a child named after a deceased relative keeps their memory alive.

The family lived in the heart of Budapest, in District VII at Klauzál Tér, which was later to be inside the Budapest Ghetto. The family lived in a typical building that featured a central enclosed courtyard, from which you could greet all the surrounding apartment dwellers on the ground floor or the upper levels. It was much the same when we visited in 2023, to be greeted by the shirtless poet, a sign one could feel that the cultural life of Budapest was continuing to thrive.

My grandfather Eli fought in the Hungarian army during World War I. Whilst his father was at the front, four-year-old Nándor would charm his way forward in the ration queues and, when he received the inadequate ration, he would join the queue again.

This cheeky and intuitive instinct for survival would serve Nándor well in World War II and would ultimately help to ensure our family's survival. Upon his return from war, Eli was granted Hungarian citizenship. A generous gesture that would save all our lives in the 1940s. Citizenship can be all-important.

The Jewish population of Budapest became the focus of rising anti-Semitism after World War I. Despite the fact that many Jews had fought in the Hungarian army, they became a target of increasing hostility. Jews outnumbered the non-Jewish population of Budapest in many areas of professional life, and anti-Semites began to call the city 'Judapest'. The term had a complex history and was used by various groups throughout the 20th century, but in 2023, there is a shop in the heart of the Jewish district which proudly welcomes people with a bold sign 'JUDAPEST'. It sells mainly Jewish-themed books and gifts made in Hungary.

After attending a Jewish school from the age of six, Misi and Nándor, like many Orthodox young men of their time, entered a yeshiva, a religious seminary, in Bratislava, Czechoslovakia. Although originally setting his sights on a secular career, Nándor continued his religious studies in Bratislava for 14 years before attaining *smicha*—his ordination as a rabbi. Although he never worked as a rabbi, Nándor remained a devoutly religious Jew throughout his life.

Meanwhile in Budapest, Nándor's sisters, my mother and Rose, left school to help support their brothers' religious studies. Women in Hungary during that period were expected to work until they married. My mother was considered intelligent, and she spoke beautiful German and English. She worked as a secretary for a man called Mr Stern, who must have thought highly of her as he employed her again, more than two decades later, in New York in the mid-1960s. He must have been an able entrepreneur to have reestablished himself in offices in the Empire State Building. Indeed, the Jewish community in Budapest was led by a Samu Stern. I conjecture: Could these connections also have helped my family's survival?

On 24 November 1940, Nándor married Edith (Pesza) Bernáth. It was considered a good match, as Pesza's father was a rabbi.

That same year, 1940, two years after returning to Hungary, Nándor was recruited by the heads of the Jewish Orthodox and Neolog communities of Budapest to be the official head of an organisation, I now think, most probably it was MIPI. MIPI was engaged in rescue and welfare work. It had been set up at the request of the American JDC which agreed to fund its work with $25,000 per month, and the Hungarians were also expected to contribute a similar amount. The JDC was a most active welfare organisation throughout the war years in Hungary as well as much of Europe and beyond, and it remains active worldwide to this day.

MIPI provided funds for both the rescue work of Kasztner and Nándor. Nándor's role involved going to the relevant foreign embassies and negotiating on behalf of the Jews he was engaged to help. From the footnotes in recorded history, he did more than just undertake the task—he fed, saved and rescued possibly countless Hungarian Jews whom I have never met but whose descendants I may yet meet. A few have made themselves known to his family.

Private family correspondence suggests that Nándor was employed by the American JDC, but that could have been through MIPI or the Hungarian Jewish Relief Committee in Budapest, set up in 1939, as JDC didn't operate openly in Budapest during World War II. Nándor was considered by the family to have enjoyed 'diplomatic' status. He had access to a car, a chauffeur and a bodyguard. He also received an income for his services. The likelihood is that he worked closely with the Swiss and/or Swedish Embassies, as I later learned. He acquired the privileges that enabled him to do his work rescuing and enabling, particularly during the most turbulent years. Like others who worked for the Swiss and Swedish Embassies, he was not required to wear the yellow star, undergo restricted movement, or be required to adhere to the curfews in 1944 and 1945, privileges which carried their own risks of danger. Privileges similar to those enjoyed by Kasztner.

Unlike elsewhere in Europe, the majority of Hungarian Jews were not in mortal danger until the spring of 1944, although the killing had begun in 1941, with Miklós Horthy's order for the roundup and deportation of 'Jewish foreign nationals'.

My mother's sister Rose was caught in the roundup of 1941. Rose had been born in Hungary, but because her parents were born in Poland, or because of the implementation of the 'racial' laws, presumably she wasn't able to produce papers proving Hungarian citizenship on demand. She paid the ultimate price.

She was one of the 18,000 deported to Kamenets-Podolsky in Ukraine. A story is told that when Nándor heard that Rose had been captured in the roundup, he quickly asked his sister-in-law Fritzi, a blonde who could pass as non-Jewish, to race to the railway station with a bag of dollars. Sadly, she was too late. Rose may have been among the victims of the two-day massacre or may have ended up on a transport to Auschwitz-Birkenau.

It was said that she did write one letter home saying that she had found a carrot to eat that tasted sweeter than any carrot she had eaten before. After that, she was not heard from again.

I am not quite sure how my aunt Rose died—the entry in Yad Vashem in Jerusalem just records: 'Deceased 1941'. It was when I was searching for her records that I first read about the horrors that befell Budapest Jews outside their country, years prior to the arrival in Budapest of the dreaded Nazi leader, Eichmann.

Some years ago, when I was in the process of writing a family memoir, I included graphic details of those massacres in 1941 when Hungarian Jews without citizenship papers on their person were herded onto trains and sent to Kamenets-Podolsky.

From the few survivors who bore witness to the event, there were reports of executions and massacres, with hundreds of people being machine-gunned down starting from 27 August. There were reported sightings of women, in rags, wearing jewellery, begging for bread with lips painted red. These were the ladies of Budapest: elegant in the face of adversity. About 15,000–16,000 were buried in the mass graves of Kamenets-Podolsky, Stanislawow, Chorkow, or thrown into gas chambers when they reached Auschwitz.

The records of the survivors in Budapest indicate the horrors of the time. Some went into hiding for nine months in attics or bunkers to escape being forced into a ghetto. Others describe themselves as wandering the whole year, from one temporary shelter to another, witnessing atrocities along the way.

One witness described a torture in which fascists cut the breasts off women, keeping them conscious long enough to see their children being sawed in two before burying them alive.

Others saw their mother and siblings shot right before their eyes. When witnesses crossed through the site of this slaughter on their way back home from the concentration camps, they found not even one single Jew alive in that place. There were no survivors.

My editor at the time thought that the stories told by the few who bore witness were too graphic to put into a family memoir. So, the graphic descriptions were deleted. But in this volume they appear as they do in the recorded testimonies of Holocaust survivors that I have had the privilege to listen to.

I have decided to include them also, as the reality has struck that man's inhumanity to man was not just a primitive historic phenomenon that played out in the 20th century, but has continued into the 21st. Despite man's ability to reach the moon, connect the globe with the World Wide Web, and identify emotions with Artificial Intelligence (AI) there is much that is primitive and inexplicably destructive.

...

From July 1941, my uncle Nándor and aunt Pesza avoided the roundups by hiding in a 'safe house' with the owner's permission. They remained there for six weeks, until it was considered safe to emerge. The family couldn't move during the day and relied on the owner's son to visit every evening with supplies. Pesza was pregnant with her first child, Robert, who arrived on 11 November of that year.

Fortunately, my parents, Sam and Etel, were in Makó at the time of the first roundups. Timing, good luck and connections played a huge role in improving chances of survival during the war. By the time my parents became aware that the authorities had started conducting document checks and deportations in country towns, they had moved back to Budapest. By then, my mother was pregnant. My older sister Judith (Judy) was born soon after, on 20 January 1942. That same month, the Germans forced Hungary to mobilise and send its troops to Russia.

Nándor worked out that bribery was the best way to gain influence with those whose support he needed. In wartime no one was above receiving inducements such as money, meat, or wood, which were offered indirectly. The family purchased goods with his personal income and then would say to the officer with whom he wanted to gain favour, 'I have been given a wagon of wood, much more than I need,' or 'Someone came to visit me from the country and brought 10 kilograms of meat, far more than I can use.' My cousin Robert recalls that his father had a Hungarian policeman helping him. Nándor used to buy him *schmaltz* (chicken or goose fat) as a bribe. Apparently, the policeman was a decent man with good intentions who was later caught by the authorities and tortured.

Nándor helped many young Jewish men avoid being drafted to join the Hungarian Labour Service System. He would inject the toxic oil of ricin into their knees to render them unfit to work. He also did this to himself, damaging his knee enough to leave him with a permanent limp. That war story was disclosed to his family. After all, his limp, although slight, was visible to others.

Another family tale concerns the time when Nándor was told there was an important individual that he should try to save during one particular roundup. He went to the man, quietly told him his plan, and gave him two bars of soap. When, as instructed, the man began to act crazed, tearing the carpet and throwing the soap against the wall, Nándor convinced the guard that he needed to be taken to hospital, from where he subsequently escaped. During wartime, all manner of approaches can help with survival.

Many years later, that man recognised Nándor in Sydney and hugged him, shouting to his family that Nándor had saved his life.

A second eminent survivor was Rabbi Akiva Sofer of Bratislava, who asked Nándor to go to the British Embassy to get a permit for him to resettle in Palestine. When Nándor successfully obtained the permit, the Rabbi asked for a second one for his son. Hard as it was to get one permit, Nándor managed to also save the Rabbi's son.

My cousin Judy (Yudka) Neuberger (née Eichel), with whom I met on my research trip to Israel, had more light to shed on these survivors. Judy believes that her father is an unsung hero of the Holocaust. She recalled stories about a woman in Sydney named Rosie Gluck, an elegant woman in the mode of exotic Hungarian actress Zsa Zsa Gabor. Rosie was a regular visitor to the Eichel home and always expressed gratitude to 'Dr Eichel' for saving her family. Judy also spoke of Mrs Reidder, an elderly woman in Manhattan, who described how Nándor had secured her exit from Budapest when she was 16 years old by arranging for her to disguise herself as a younger child.

Nándor had procured a visa to Israel for the Chief Rabbi of Belz and arranged for the Rabbi to live with his in-laws, the Bernáth family, until he could leave Budapest. The Belz Rabbi, who was known as Aharon Rokeach, was indeed on one of those trains to Strasshof. Nándor may have had a lot to do with those trains. After all, some of my Makó family were also on the trains that ended up in Strasshof. It is easy to imagine that the saving of rabbis had become an important part of the conversation in a religious household, as a matter of pride and significance.

When Nándor saw long queues at the various consulates, he would call ahead and explain that he was the representative of an American charity, most likely the JDC which paid the funds to MIPI. He would then receive a letter for entry so that he could avoid the queues. His affable personality allowed him to gain favour with the consular officials whose support he needed. In particular, he enjoyed a good relationship with Carl Lutz, the Swiss ambassador.

Part 2

*'Train yourself never to put off the word or action
for the expression of gratitude.'*

—Albert Schweitzer

Chapter Five
One Budapesti Schindler

Carl Lutz

During the occupation of Hungary by the Nazis in World War II, many notable heroes came to light, but the name 'Carl Lutz' does not spring to mind for many people. But it should.

Lutz has been described as a Swiss version of Oskar Schindler. During his tenure as Swiss Vice-Consul in Budapest, he helped close to 10,000 Jewish children emigrate from Nazi-occupied Hungary. He is said to have saved over 62,000 Jews in total.

Lutz is considered to have saved perhaps more than any other man in the months of the German occupation of Budapest. At war's end he was disciplined rather than lauded by his superiors for his daring feats. Recognition came much later.

In the public eye Lutz's efforts remain in the shadow of the Swedish diplomat, Raoul Wallenberg, who achieved world fame with his actions over six months whilst in Budapest in 1944-1945, and whose fate was a tragic one.

As World War II raged in Europe, Hitler's Nazi regime was delivering literally millions of Jews in cattle trucks and trains to their torturous deaths by bullets or gas in extermination camps. Meanwhile, in Budapest and Hungary, Jews were somewhat safer. The greatest risk was for able-bodied Jewish men—if that was you, you would not be drafted into the Hungarian army but rather drafted and sent for labour service in Ukraine, in harsh conditions from which few men returned.

There were a great number of Jewish refugees from neighbouring countries such as Poland, Slovakia, Austria, to name a few, who managed to cross into Hungary and Romania in the hope of finding food, shelter, and perhaps a visa to the British territory of Palestine. So, the offices where Rezső Kasztner worked in supporting the refugees were busy in aid and rescue. As was the embassy of the neutral country of Switzerland.

As Europe was in the grip of war, and the extermination of Jews was at catastrophic levels by 1944, the Jewish population of Hungary had generally been spared from Hitler's 'Final Solution' for ridding Europe of its entire Jewish population.

Adolf Hitler was, for a time, more than happy with the Hungarians' behaviour as a model ally. They were supplying troops for the invasions of Yugoslavia and the Soviet Union, so he left Hungary alone.

But the Hungarians had been conducting secret armistice negotiations with the Allies behind the Führer's back which raised the ire of Hitler. Germany invaded Hungary in March 1944, and the country was annexed to the Third Reich.

It did not take long for the Germans to put the 'Final Solution to the Jewish Question' into full effect. Something they did with great speed and efficiency. Tens of thousands of Jews, Roma, and other Nazi-decreed undesirables were rounded up and deported to the extermination camp at Auschwitz.

The use of visas to prevent the deportation of Jews had occurred elsewhere in places such as France, but in Budapest, they were used most effectively to save the largest number of people. Despite the rapid extermination of the Jewish population, the number of people who were rescued through the use of documentation such as visas was considered to be the highest in Budapest.

In addition to issuing passports and visas, Carl Lutz and his wife also hoisted the Swiss flag above houses to place their inhabitants under diplomatic protection, an action also taken by other ambassadors, like Raoul Wallenberg.

Despite the close alliance with Nazi Germany, the Hungarian government under Regent Miklós Horthy had previously refused to conduct mass deportations. Bowing to international pressure, he didn't want to jeopardise his negotiating powers if and when the Axis powers were defeated, which he believed would happen. He wanted to be able to negotiate effectively with the Allies. However, after the German invasion, mass deportation was implemented without wasting time, and at the same time, with great brutality.

The Jewish population of Hungary was estimated to be approximately 825,000 in 1944. About 565,000 were considered to have been murdered in Auschwitz. Within the space of a mere 56 days or 7 weeks, 424,000 were deported.

The German occupation in Hungary was similar as that of Denmark. Despite the presence of German troops, the Hungarian government was not dismantled after the German invasion. The Hungarian state functioned almost as before. One big exception was the immediate setting up of Councils of Jewish leaders, known as Judenräte, to facilitate the implementation of Nazi policies.

In this complex climate of war, intrigue, brutality and machination, there were good men going about their business, using whatever powers they had available to them. The diplomats of neutral countries wielded influence.

Carl Lutz was one such diplomat.

•••

Lutz was born into a Methodist family in Walzenhausen in the Swiss mountains of the canton Appenzell Ausserrhoden on 30 March 1895. He has been described as the archetypical Swiss man in that he was a multi-faceted character. He was introverted and religious, and at the same time he was bold and adventurous.

His father owned a sandstone quarry in Appenzell. His mother died of tuberculosis when he was 14 years old. At the age of 15 he began to work in a textile mill but by the time he was 18 in 1913, he had moved to the USA where he first worked to support himself through college and subsequently worked there for more than 20 years.

His first role was in the Swiss Consular Corps at the Swiss Legation in Washington DC in 1920. By 1926 he rose in rank and became Chancellor of the Swiss Consulate in Philadelphia, and later in St Louis. In 1934, he met his first wife, Gertrud Fankhauser. They were married in 1935 after he left the USA and became the Swiss Consulate General in Jaffa (which was then the British Mandate of Palestine). It was in Jaffa where he would encounter hatred towards the Jews for the first time, when he and his wife witnessed from their apartment building an unarmed Jew being lynched by an Arab mob.

He served there till 1942.

It was following the experience in Jaffa in 1942 that he took a posting in Budapest where he became the Swiss Vice-Consul to Hungary. Cooperation with neutral Switzerland was sought after, to assist with refugees and as a representative of the allied countries whose interests needed care in the context of war. He was able to represent the diplomatic interests of states that were at war with Hungary. The Swiss legation was tasked to look after the interests of their citizens. Initially there were 10 of these states, which later became as many as 14, the most important being the United States of America, Great Britain, Belgium, Yugoslavia, Egypt, Chile, Central and South American countries, including El Salvador and Honduras.

Lutz had friends in the diplomatic communities of United States, United Kingdom, and Germany and that made him a very good choice for his ever-expanding role.

By 1944, the American Embassy in Budapest was abandoned so Lutz was located in the American Embassy's 22-room office building with more than 100 staff to manage the Swiss Embassy's commitments. The site of the building in Szabadság (Freedom) Square had featured on many occasions in Hungary's 20th-century history, with protests and celebrations alternating at different times over the years. Eight decades later, we were able to experience the sense of freedom as tourists when we visited here in 2023, unlike our experience of insecurity and restraint in a sombre environment when we visited during the Communist era in the late 1960s and early 1980s.

Lutz got to know others who were involved in assisting with emigration like Miklós Krausz who had headed the Palestinian Bureau in Budapest since 1934, and Rezső Kasztner who was a leader in the Aid and Rescue Committee. And, most likely, Nándor Eichel was another local operator whom these men would have dealt with. Indeed, because there is a lack of clarity as to who Nándor's direct employer was at the time, he may have been a subordinate to one of these men or at least associated with them in a work relationship. Given Kasztner's fate post-war, it is not so surprising that Nándor remained both silent and evasive about his wartime employment.

In the midst of war, when those who were found to forge documents were arrested, Lutz tried to maintain correct relationships with everyone. He carefully observed the rules of diplomacy. He regularly sought approval for his actions from his superior, Ambassador Jaeger, who wrote a glowing report about him, and reported changes of plans to the Swiss Ministry of Foreign Affairs and to the neutral missions in Budapest—the Vatican, Sweden and Switzerland, and any other embassies that were involved in any particular decision.

***

It is not too difficult to imagine walking in Lutz's shoes, looking after people, following procedures to the letter as a diplomat—lives were at stake, but rules were to be adhered to. For others, rules were to be ignored during the chaos of war when bribery and using whatever means necessary were accepted practices. Moving around in wartime Budapest was in itself risky, but making sure you could stay in your post by following the rules of diplomacy would also have been vitally important. His Swedish counterpart, Raoul Wallenberg, who arrived some three years later, seems to have been more of a risk-taker and demanding of latitude from his superiors. The men were different, and Lutz seems to have been a highly effective negotiator. His capacity for work seems to have been amazing and he appears to have remained at 'arm's length' from illegal activities.

While the rescue of Jews was not part of Lutz's original job description, it became a major part of his life's work. He played a critical role in rescue activities by claiming diplomatic immunity for 72 protected houses established around Budapest, and by issuing no less than 62,000 protection certificates to Jews, thereby saving the lives of nearly half the Jewish population of Budapest. Each certificate or *Schutzpasse* stated that the holder was deemed to be in the protectorate of Switzerland. He also successfully negotiated the emigration of 10,000 Jews to Palestine. By 1944 he represented 13 countries in addition to Switzerland, including the United States.

One of the houses Lutz arranged to be protected with political immunity was in Vadász Street. Known as the Glass House, (Üvegház) it became the headquarters for the coordinated rescue and relief activities for the Jews of Budapest. Up to 3,000 Jews took refuge in the Glass House in the autumn of 1944 and the winter of 1944-1945.

The owners of the Glass House, the Weiss family, had it built as a glass plant and shop. It was chosen because it was close to the Swiss Embassy, enabling a quick getaway when needed. Jewish Zionist youth did their illegal and dangerous work in the house, producing certificates and delivering them. The Palestine Office also took refuge there. It was attacked three times during the war, first by the police and twice by the Arrow Cross Party.

However, the Glass House survived and stands to this day.

The country boy

I was reminded of Andor Schwarz's description of his personal journey during those months in Budapest in 1944, how he had come from a wealthy family that had lived in a castle to becoming a streetwise teenager on the run. Like many

Holocaust survivors, Andor Schwartz also chose to remain silent—at least on the printed page—until late in life, when his 80th birthday was nearing. It was then that he chose to record his story, which he did in great detail.

Andor had never been to Budapest till May 1944. He described how he had arrived in Újpest, meaning literally 'New Pest', which was then considered to be on the outskirts of the city but which formally became a district in Budapest in 1950. In his 2003 memoir, *Living Memory*, he describes how, after leaving Újpest, he was on the run from house to house. Word had spread that the Glass House in the 7th District was operating as a safe haven for Jews. On 14th October he arrived there after 8 pm in search of a bed when the doors were already closed and the House was at 'full' capacity. Undeterred, young Andor was bold, brave, and handsome, even when on the run—he describes how he managed to get inside to ask for help as he approached the young woman at the desk:

> *I told her I was a country boy and had never been in Budapest before and didn't know what Budapest looked like. I asked if I could stay there just for the night and tomorrow, I would move.*

She said 'No' but reneged upon seeing his 'painful' face. Inside, he explored the two-story building, with office spaces on the ground floor opening to a warehouse area where covered stores of shelving displayed neatly packed glasses of all shapes, sizes, and colours, all arranged in perfect order. Amongst them, he found many people seeking refuge, mostly from Budapest, the 'top-notch of the city'. The Zionist youth who were busily working at forging Palestinian entry certificates and rescue work in Budapest, had bunkered down in the cellar under the warehouses. On the top floor of the building were the offices of the Weiss family, in which Arthur Weiss, the Honorary Swiss Consul, worked.

Andor recounts his experiences vividly despite more than six decades having passed. He describes noticing the daughter of the owner, Mr Weiss, who, along with the family, had some living quarters upstairs despite their main home being elsewhere. He fell in love with the owner's daughter and enjoyed the luxury of her company, food, and conversation.

He did not stay for just one night, but rather was able to talk his way into becoming a porter at the Glass House. That meant delivering messages and 'freedom passes' to all who had the good fortune to get one. He worked several shifts, some from midnight till 8 am, which involved watching the door, while outside the safe house life in Budapest became ever more dangerous.

On 15 October, the Germans took Budapest from Horthy through a coup and sent him to Germany, but after the war he ended up in exile in Portugal.[1] The streets filled with SS soldiers, and the Arrow Cross under Ferenc Szálasi's leadership had taken over as Nazi enforcers. Andor heard that the Arrow Cross had a quota of Jews they had to kill each day. As they found them, they were herded to the edge of the Danube and gunned into the waters. As Andor recalled: 'The Street was a death trap. You could stay outside only until the Arrow Cross thugs arrived, then that would be the end of you.'

Every building in the city seemed to have its own Arrow Cross caretaker, with a room at street level. In the main they were unsympathetic to Jews and would watch to see that no Jew entered. If one tried to enter, they would be seized, detained, and handed over to the Arrow Cross. They were considered worse than the SS, a statement my own parents were heard to say on more than one occasion. Andor, however, articulated that the SS wouldn't kill you on the street, but would arrest people for deportation and the death camps; the Arrow Cross would shoot Jews on sight, kicking the bodies to the side of the footpath. According to Andor,

> *It was the beginning of November; the street became bloodier and bloodier. All the Jews of the city were living in the ghetto, mostly old men, and women. The young people, if any were around, were in hiding. The Arrow Cross had started to clear out the Swedish*

> *protected homes. Nothing helped any more. The food in Vadász Street became less and less (and) as I stood in the doorway, people were still daring to come to the door and begging to be let in. I didn't care anymore—I just let them in. By then there were two thousand of us suffering there.*

Jewish people clamoured to get into the Glass House—one of the few places of refuge. And one of the only chances for escape and a good chance of survival through the use of Schutzpasse, or Schutz brief, which claimed that the holder of the document was under the protection of a particular country, such as Switzerland. Inside, the secretary and another helper were writing names on these documents. The passes were already printed with the large, round red stamps of the Swiss Embassy of Budapest, which made it possible for the holder to cross the border and make an escape to Switzerland as soon as possible.

The images of that building being overwhelmed with people six- and 10-deep trying to gain access are frequently seen on the internet to illustrate how desperate people were at that time to find support for shelter, exit visas, or for anything else that might help them to survive. At least that was the picture in the early days of the Glass House; that is, after July 1944, before the reign of terror of the Arrow Cross that Andor Schwartz describes. By October it was not safe to be in the streets.

> *Later on, in the middle of November, the transports stopped as the road towards Germany was cut off by the Russians, but still the killing went on ... By then the Schutzpass wasn't of much value. There had been too many issued. The Swedes also had the same scheme. Theirs was of better value as Wallenberg, the Swedish Ambassador, personally acted to take all the people who had protective papers out of the wagons. The Swedes also had their safe houses. ... These safe houses protected you in the beginning, although if the Nazis wanted*

to go inside nobody could hold them back. The law was in the mob's hands. After November 15th or 18th everything changed. Papers and safe houses became worthless and no longer safe. You had to be lucky to survive.

Stepping into the Glass House

In late June 2023 I walk into what remains in existence today as the Glass House Museum, 29 Vadász Street, (Vadász utca), Budapest. It is also known as the Glass House Documentation and Memorial Center. The model of the 1944 building stands in the centre of the room, showing how 3,000 people could be layered onto makeshift wooden slats to sleep in one large room.

Decades later, I take in the experience of being in that building, nothing special by today's Budapesti standards, but there is a courtyard, and there is grass growing in a modest space that must have been a safe sanctuary for thousands. For me, it was a way of coming close to the reality of what must have been.

It is set deep amongst what is now known as Budapest's 'ruin bars' culture, in old buildings in the Jewish Quarter known for their quirky décor and lively atmosphere. We went to several. We ate at hip restaurants and ate street food in a place known as the Karavan. It is now a widely enjoyed tourist environment that bears little signs of its more horrendous past. The echoes of the past are only evident when one searches for them, such as people choosing to inform themselves through visiting a museum or reading historical texts, or even novels by contemporary authors.[2] But it is the Glass House that bears significance and moves me.

Inside the building there is displayed a letter addressed to 'Dear Mr Consul.' It is an expression of deepest warm-hearted gratitude ' … to you for what you have done for us and for exerting those arduous efforts so generously in our interest' by ex-Regent Horthy on 7 July 1947. For the work of the Swiss consulate, 'how cordially you looked after us with utmost care. In these days of hard and critical times for the human race, when one is unexpectedly disappointed by many, one can be filled with double joy, when good old friends free from deceitful propaganda recognise the real situation.'

Miklós Horthy was indeed a complex character with a mixed reputation. He was known to have meted out harsh treatment of those under his command in 1914, praised for his foreign policy between the two World Wars and for his ambition to regain control of territory lost in World War 1. As Regent, he raised the ire of Hitler in 1944, and then he wrote the words of appreciation for what the Swiss Consul had done in the protection of Hungarians in 1944.

Like many powerful historical artifacts that one comes across decades later, it is not difficult to imagine the author sitting at his desk writing on plain letterhead, without title, making a statement—or indeed an *understatement* of gratitude to the Swiss Consul. After all, at the end of the war, Carl Lutz had made an endless number of decisions without authorisation, and taken risks in protecting countless people, but he was not welcomed as a hero—rather ignored by his own community. In fact, immediately after the war he was criticised by the Swiss Government who feared he'd endangered their steadfast national policy of neutrality. The apology was to come much later.

Lutz was a modest man, a trait that perhaps stemmed from his humble beginnings in the small town of Walzenhausen in Switzerland where he was keen to escape the boredom. He was considered to be bold and daring in action, but willing to share accolades and recognitions by giving credit to others at war's end.

Lutz's quiet and humble personality style may have served him well in those turbulent times, as he did not suffer the same fate as the much lauded and acknowledged Budapesti Schindler, Wallenberg, who was taken away at war's end, whereabouts to this day unknown. Wallenberg has been lauded by biographers and historians, but it is Lutz who has been credited with the methods used by other diplomats, like Wallenberg, who learnt from him.[3]

Lutz's methods with production and distribution of the protection passports, official or otherwise, undeniably worked. How he was able to sway the Hungarian authorities to approve those passes is a question asked by many over the years. The answer is not complex and involves Lutz recognising and negotiating within a political climate that allowed for the passes to operate as a protection for the holder. The Hungarian authorities became increasingly pragmatic as German military defeat became more likely. They were looking for ways to mitigate the reputational disaster that being seen to cooperate with the Nazi's genocidal mission risked, which meant they were willing to work with humanitarians, if only to further their own goals. The minutes from the Council of Ministers of the time attest to this:

> *It is my impression that the position of the Hungarian Cabinet regarding the interest of neutral and foreign parties will bring about a decisive influence on the Hungarian nation's international relations not only during the war but for a long time to come. Hungary's planned radical solution is a heavy burden to Hungary and to the Hungarian government, which will bring unavoidable disadvantages in international relations during the war ... after the war as countries remain in the community of nations many will recommend breaking diplomatic ties with Hungary. The Hungarian people will have such a heavy burden to bear ...*
>
> *To prevent this, I may be so bold as to advise the Council of Ministers to create an opening whereby we could reduce the aforementioned tension and in that way create a tolerable atmosphere in our international relations.*[4]

Hungary was worried about reprisals. It was thought that the countries that the passholder was representing would take revenge if they did not treat their citizens well. The Germans had experienced reversals on the front lines, and the Allies could see that the war was nearing its end. There was international political pressure from the USA which was threatening postwar reprisals. Hungary considered its relations with neutral Switzerland and Sweden important, with a need to maintain significant economic ties to both countries. Not to mention the esteem that Hungary had for the Vatican. Hungary was a Catholic country with the Vatican playing a role in the lives of many Hungarians.

Those amazing feats—safe houses and citizenship visas—*did* work. The results: the tangible fact that many Hungarian Jews did escape the worst ravages of the Holocaust. This is indisputable. How exactly it happened is a fascinating question. In the midst of the horror of the final year of the war there was great potential for deadly damage to be done. But it was the Budapesti Schindlers, ambassadors and unofficial diplomats, who had the creativity and capacity to successfully convince the governing authorities to accept their protective passes, at least for some months. It is difficult to discern who had the inspiration to game the system, or who was the most influential negotiator.

Perhaps the best known of the Budapesti Schindlers was the previously mentioned Swedish Ambassador, Raoul Wallenberg, who has been recognised for his great work but who was a victim of the Soviet Regime. His disappearance at the time of the Cold War was thought to be used as propaganda against the Soviet Union. More about him later, but needless to say, Wallenberg was working and benefitting from the same favourable government decrees that recognised both his and Lutz's ambassadorial activities.

And there are others, such as Angelo Rotta, Papal delegate; and his closest colleague Gennaro Verolino; the Swiss Friedrich Born working in the name of the Red Cross; and Valdemar Langlet and his wife, Nina, working in the name of the Swedish Red Cross, along with the Spanish and Portuguese ambassadors.[5] In the heat of the war period, when there was so much to be done, many individuals were doing quite amazing work. Some have been lauded in various places.

Another question that is frequently directed at the Hungarian experience: How did the Hungarian Jews not know what was happening in the death camps of neighbouring Poland?

It's perhaps difficult to understand, in today's overheated mediascape, just how efficacious the Nazis and their allies were at controlling information. One example of their exemplary control of the narrative was when the Red Cross visited Auschwitz and other concentration camps, they were shown carefully sanitised and selected models of imprisonment. They walked away satisfied that human rights were not being violated. This is regarded as perhaps the greatest single failing in the history of the Red Cross, serving as evidence of the Nazi's complete control of the narrative of the time.

While the extermination of Jews and others was being executed on a large scale, gas and crematoria were banned from official records. Every SS guard and officer at Auschwitz had signed a pledge that they would not discuss their work, even with their co-workers. The punishment for spreading 'horror stories' was execution. There was practically no communication between Budapest and the provinces.

There was nothing in the newspapers or on the BBC, and no mention in the American media.

In any case, Jews were not permitted to have radios. The Hungarian language Jewish newspaper *Új Kelet*, published in Kolozsvár (now Cluj-Napoca) had long been shut down, as were all Jewish newspapers in 1941. What reporting there was, even for those who could obtain or assemble a clandestine radio, did not reflect the realities of the situation.

For example, when the Nazi tanks rolled in on 19 March 1944, Radio Budapest kept broadcasting light music with selections of Mozart and Strauss. Only the BBC announced the occupation. The Government of Miklós Kállay was dissolved, and the Prime Minister had fled, begging asylum from Turkey. Döme Sztójay, Hungary's former ambassador to Germany, was named Prime Minister. Horthy was allowed to stay on as Regent, on the understanding that he would cooperate with Hitler. The news of the war, in a general sense, was transmitted on the BBC, when one could get access to a radio; however by April 1st there was a ban on listening to foreign radio stations.

Eichmann himself arrived on 21 March and began to implement the *dejudification* (clearance of Jews) program. By then Eichmann had visited Bergen-Belsen, Auschwitz, and Dachau camps, so he knew what was happening. He had sent 380 trainloads of French to the east, most of the Jews in Poland had been murdered, and the Jews of Western Russia and Ukraine and Holland had been slaughtered. As the German saying went, he was after 'efficiency with gas'.

On March 22, only three days after the occupation, there were nine anti-Jewish decrees passed in Hungary. Jews were denied sugar, shortening, had to surrender summer homes, and books by Jewish authors were banned in the libraries. Radios had to be surrendered. Jews would have to wear yellow stars to identify them as such in public.

There must have been an extraordinary sense of disbelief and a call to action.

***

At dawn on March 27, Rezső Kasztner went to Carl Lutz, the consul occupying the US Embassy in Szabadság (Liberty) Square. The Swiss were representing United States interests in Hungary, and Lutz had also represented German interests in the Middle East, where, during his service in Palestine, he had Germans sent to safety after Germany had declared war on Great Britain. This explains why Lutz was somewhat respected by the Germans, and so was well placed to do his work in Budapest at that time.

Kasztner was met by a sea of people packed into the building. He went straight upstairs to Lutz's large office where two men, Miklós (Moshe) Krausz, of the Palestine Office of the Jewish Agency in Budapest, and Ottó Komoly, the president of the Budapest Zionist association, were already there. Lutz, still in his 40s, was dapper, tall, thin and wearing wire-rimmed glasses. Krausz and Komoly were unkempt and looked like they had not slept.

Lutz told Kasztner that the Jewish Agency's Palestine Office should be transferred to the Swiss legation. And that is how Lutz got to work with Krausz. Krausz was worried about papers and stamps which had been taken by the police. The police and youth wearing Arrow Cross armbands prowled outside. Kasztner called Krausz 'a fussy little cockroach'[6] for worrying about papers at a time like this. Krausz was to be set up in the basement, and the department was to be renamed the Emigration Department.

Needless to say, the relationship between the two men was never good.

The bombings began

On 3 April 1944, British and American aircraft began the unremitting bombing of Budapest. Buildings collapsed in the arteries to the city and in Buda. The Jewish Council was asked to provide 500 apartments for Christians who were affected by the raids, while Jews were relocated to the National Theatre or the Dohány Street Synagogue.

There is uncertainty about what people knew, or did not know, as to the fate of the Jews in the Polish concentration camps. Two young Slovakians, Rudolf Vrba and Alfréd Wetzler (born in the Kingdom of Hungary who later lived in Slovakia) escaped from Auschwitz-Birkenau on 7 April, 1944, and have been credited with detailing the horrors, to raise the alarm with a factual account of what was happening with the building and usage of the crematoria in Auschwitz. The document known as the *Auschwitz Protocols* was translated into English and German within a few weeks. Rezső Kasztner had been in Bratislava, where he delivered badly needed American dollars and returned to Budapest with a copy of the protocols.

Oskar Schindler had warned Kasztner of those horrors when they met, but receiving the document that was being shared with authorities (the Slovakians had sent the document to the Red Cross and the United States) brought it home as an undeniable reality. Kasztner wanted the document translated into Hungarian in case the nuances of what seemed unbelievable would change. He shared the document with Samu Stern who was leading the operations in Budapest as the head of the National Bureau of Hungarian Jews.

On 29 April 1944, the first transport of 1,800 persons left for the notorious extermination camp of Auschwitz-Birkenau, while Lutz and countless others worked around the clock to mitigate further genocide. Wallenberg was yet to arrive.

On 5 May, Kasztner[7] crossed the Chain Bridge to take the protocols to Lutz's residence in the beautiful 19th-century manor house in Old Buda, the former location of the British legation in Hungary.

He was met by the butler and offered chilled wine which he didn't accept despite being parched from his long haul across the bridge and up the hill. Kasztner stood in the window overlooking the river whilst Lutz read the document. The room the men spoke in, with its chandeliers, was in stark contrast to what was described in the papers. Indeed, the whole scene in that beautiful hilltop location overlooking the still, tranquil river Danube, brought for those present the sharp awareness of the unbelievable horror and reality of what was on those pages.

The shock and fury led Lutz to call for his car, and together with Kasztner, the men went to Moshe Krausz's new office at the former American Embassy. It was an urgent matter—the life and death of many hundreds of thousands was at stake. By 15 May, trains would be crossing through Slovakia and southern Poland, and within two weeks the north of Hungary would be free of Jews.

Lutz asked the Swiss minister whether he could send the protocols to Berne and was told 'No'—it was not considered to be good for a neutral country to mix in the affairs of other countries.

So, in June 1944, Krausz sent the *Auschwitz Protocols*, probably with Lutz's knowledge, from Budapest to Geneva with the information about extermination camps. The Swiss public was outraged. A Swiss press campaign generated an estimated 400 headlines protesting the atrocities against civilians. Swiss churches advocated the plight of the Jewish people, and large-scale public demonstrations drew global attention.

> Allied leaders singled out the Hungarian state for their role in atrocities:
> Winston Churchill said, as recorded in *Hansard,* 26 June, 1944:
>
> *There is no doubt that the murder of the Hungarian Jews is ... the greatest and most horrible crime ever committed in the whole history of the world, and it has been done by scientific machinery by nominally civilized men in the name of a great State and one of the leading races of Europe.*

Faced with an international public relations crisis, the Hungarian authorities began to look for ways to mitigate the punishment that would likely find them in the event of an Allied victory. Horthy's regime—probably more out of self-interested pragmatism than compassion, noted by others such as historian Oszvath—became more receptive to avenues of escape for the Jews of Hungary. In Budapest, those who *could* act began to search for unorthodox ways to navigate the system, and save lives.

In June 1944, after three months of negotiations between Kasztner and the SS, a payment of a huge ransom to secure the safety of Hungarian Jews was agreed. On 30 June the 35-car train with 1,684 passengers departed from Budapest's Rákosrendező train station for the West. The journalist, György Vámos, who wrote extensively about this period, particularly about the activities of Carl Lutz at the Glass House, claims that the fate of the train depended on the work of the Palestine Bureau, which included Lutz and Krausz. According to Vámos, both the rescue efforts and the Krausz/Lutz protections were initiated by the Rescue Committee, as the starting points were the Palestinian entry certificates.

Krausz got the certificates, and Kasztner negotiated with Eichmann. The two men didn't like each other, and, again according to Vámos, Kraus's style under pressure and his personality were upsetting to the young volunteers who were working in the basement of the Glass House after 24 July.

How the diplomatic passes came into being

Initially, neutral diplomats sought to primarily ensure the security of the non-Hungarian citizens, including Jews of the countries they represented. These could avoid legal restrictions and deportations.

As the situation worsened, they started developing various kinds of identity and protection documents. Swedish documents similar to the Swiss ones were provided to individuals and their relatives who had family in Sweden or pursued business relations with that country. The pass read:

> *The Swedish Royal Legation has the honour to request all relevant Authorities, in matters concerning the named individual, to give favourable consideration to the circumstances of the individual is permitted to enter Sweden as soon as travel is possible.*

In late June, protection documents from other countries began to appear, such as the Vatican, El Salvador, Portugal, and the International Red Cross.

The Swiss gave badges to staff members, which included a number of Hungarian Jews who were exempt from having to wear a yellow star, much like the foreign diplomats. There was lengthy debate about all this, but it was approved by Regent Horthy. Hungarian employees of the diplomatic corps received identification documents. Nándor Eichel would have had such privileges, allowing him freedom of movement, access to a car and chauffeur, and exemption from curfews when they were evoked.

At that point, Jews were not under immediate threat of deportation because Regent Horthy stopped deportations for a couple of months as Nazi control began to wane. However, it was when the notorious Arrow Cross (Nyilas) came into power that the Palestinian visa became most useful.

Lutz had convinced the Hungarians that the granting of visas and exemptions would put Hungary in favour as an international citizen, and in doing so, avoid air strikes. The cabinet approved the idea, and as long as the Allies dealt favourably with the Hungarian nationals, and vice versa, the ideas were acceptable.

The Hungarians wanted to improve the international perception of the country after the backlash following media reports of German atrocities. Thus, at the 25 June cabinet meeting, the Swiss legation had made the request, arguing that this would be a good way to avoid strikes from Allies. The cabinet meeting of 5 July approved the decision and approved the announcement a week later. Meanwhile, by 9 July, 26 additional transports left for Auschwitz.

On 3 August, Lutz reported that emigration of 8,000 Jews had been confirmed. Apparently, total chaos reigned, and Lutz announced that he had issued more than 22,000 protection letters.[8]

By July the office space in Szabadság Square was not big enough to deal with so many thousands of requests, and the Lutz team was forced to look for other space. That was when the wholesale glass material building owned by the Weiss family in Vadász street was proposed—built in the early 1930s, it served as a showroom for construction industry glassware products. The bright and shiny building by the summer of 1944 was no longer in use, and was suitable for its new purpose as a place of refuge. It was leased from Weiss, and in return, Weiss asked to be on the émigré list. The Weiss family lived at 23 Pozsonyi Street. The family were on the first group passport and survived the war, that is, except for Weiss himself who became a victim of the Hungarian holocaust.

The Glass House was officially opened for diplomatic business on 24 July and set up with the sign outside reading: *Emigration Section of the Office for Foreign Interests Representation of the Swiss Legation.*

Arthur Weiss organised the building as he would have run an embassy: by function. Such as, for example, the admissions area, the reception area, and the ground floor offices of the employees. It was here that the Glass House team were able to distribute passes and collective passports, vital to the survival of so many Hungarians.

The collective passport resembled a folder with a letter typewritten in German and French:

> *Office for Foreign Interests Representation of the Swiss Legation requests all civil and military authorities to grant free and unrestricted passage and transit to all persons recognized in this collective passport. Our Representation recommends that support and protection for these persons to be given by all authorities and officials inasmuch as such a request is presented to the esteemed authorities.*

Next to Lutz's signature was placed the enormous Legation seal in red wax. The counsellor of the Hungarian Interior Ministry appended the following handwritten document: I grant permission for the persons listed with numbers 1 through to 967 in collective passport No. 1, dated July 29 and issued by the Swiss Legation in Budapest, to exit the country by August 25, 1944, Budapest, July 31, 1944.[9]

In the following weeks three similar passports were completed. The people named on the group passport received a half-page German-language document whose letterhead featured the Office for Foreign Interests Representation of the Swiss Legation. The document certified that these persons were registered on the official list of émigrés to Palestine.

Once word got around about the possibility of these visas, the lines of people desperate to apply snaked along Vadász Street. This was despite the danger posed from strict restrictions on Jews being out in the streets.

Transit visas were needed for each country involved in the journey. By 1 August, the Romanian transit visa was available. Ships were to be in Constanta, the Romanian port, by 10 August, but German permission was required. Himmler wanted to avoid conflict with another ally, so he gave instructions that the Hungarian wish be honoured. However, the Germans issued the permission for transit visas for émigré groups only on 15 November, by which time the Red Army had already occupied half of Hungary.

By the summer, the Glass House was a centre for the distribution of forged documents—couriers delivered them. The building's status as a hub for refugees was an open secret in Budapest. That is how the streetwise Andor Schwarz and those seeking shelter and documents to secure their safety heard about it. An August article in the paper *Magyar Szó* (Hungarian Word) reported that the office in Vadász Street was a 'centre for underground emigration' and 'The Glass House in Vadász Street is today a source of infection which should be destroyed and exterminated.'

People lived full-time in the Glass House—workers sleeping between shifts, mainly working from the basement to maintain the illusion that the building was unoccupied. They slept alongside those who had escaped from labour camps.

Upon entry one would see offices, then the work rooms, then the storeroom, the attic, and the basements. Young guards controlled the admittance at the entrance. In the large ground-floor room was the information desk; in the second-floor office were the assistants who received the applications during the day and slept on the desks at night.

Next door at Vadász Street 31 was the Hungarian Football Association. When they moved out, the overflow from the Glass Factory moved in. The relatively modest building was soon packed to the rafters with people, and an ersatz Jewish community sprang up.

'A thin slice of bread and a big portion of liverwurst' was how one person remembered the food. They dug a latrine in the courtyard, and with a few faucets of water, a huge washtub was placed in the attic. Guests washed from the waist up and hung shirts out to dry which froze in the cold. An infirmary was set up, but luckily, no epidemic illness broke out. A choir and Hebrew lessons were organised.

After 23 October, Swiss protection letters were being issued *en masse* and delivered to tens of thousands of Jews. The international ghetto was set up in the Pozsonyi Street neighbourhood consisting of protective houses of the Swiss, the Swedish, Spanish, Portuguese, and Vatican missions. The residents of these missions were assisted by the Glass House operations in practical matters such as repairs and plumbing.

Carl Lutz must have been fearless and has been described as 'indefatigable.' The story is told of how he drove to the Danube and, in front of the Arrow Cross, jumped into the river to save a bleeding Jewish woman who had been shot by the Arrow Cross. With water up to his neck, he swam back with her and faced the firing squad, declaring that the wounded woman was a foreign citizen under Swiss protection. He was forthright and authoritative and left the fascists stunned. He was tall and eloquent, and no one seemed to have stopped him. The quay now bears his name, *Carl Lutz Rakpart*.

It is difficult to imagine how risky it was for an individual—even a powerful, well-connected individual—to stand up to armed fascists. It was dangerous diplomacy. Other Budapesti Schindlers were not so lucky.

The Fall of the Glass House

New Year's Eve, 1944: Lutz was stuck on Castle Hill when the biggest raid on the Glass House took place, and the front entrance was blown up. Weiss was taken to City Hall, beaten, and then shot at the Danube—a pair of ghostly shoes that are part of the memorial sculpture that rests on the bank today may well be his, or any of those who lost their lives, or the few who managed to crawl out of the water, shoeless.

Andor Schwartz vividly describes one of those raids. One morning, around November, he heard unusual noises from the street when the Arrow Cross arrived at the Glass House door, hammering on it with their gun butts, yelling for them to open up:

> *I thought there was not much use in refusing to open it as they could just toss a hand grenade in the doorway. It would be open in a much bigger way. So, I opened the door in front of me and there were at least fifty Arrow Cross Nazis from the Danube squad standing outside. I was picked up by a large 'animal', held up high and tossed against the wall. I collapsed there for a minute. I wasn't hit with a gun like the rest. I wasn't wounded. They ran into the yard, shouting and ordering everybody out into the street. They pushed nearly a thousand people outside, but they didn't find the three Zionist bunkers [the volunteer youth workers]. Everybody had to turn to the wall with their hands up high touching the wall. I was also outside looking right and left. There was no escape as both sides of the street were closed and the whole street was full of them running up and down. I knew we would soon walk to the Danube.*

As Andor contemplated his likely imminent death, he heard a commotion break out. Looking back into the street, he saw Arthur Weiss striding out of the Glass House. The Arrow Cross knew who he was and let him pass without violence. Weiss walked up to the leader of the death squad, who was sitting in a car in the middle of the street, and stated firmly, 'This place belongs to the Swiss Consulate. You have no right to drive those people out.'

A heated argument ensued during which Arthur Weiss rang an army general who arrived promptly, along with staff from the Swiss Embassy. Throughout the argument, Andor looked for an opportunity to make a break for it, but in the end, Weiss seemed to win the argument. The Arrow Cross let the Jews they'd taken hostage return to the Glass House, but told Arthur Weiss that he should leave with them, that is, for the Arrow Cross leadership to sort things out. He was taken away and murdered.[10] When he died, so did the hope for thousands of Jews, with little chance of escape without him. He too should carry the title, a Budapesti Schindler.

Schwarz wrote:

> *After Mr Weiss's death the place became like a body with the head cut off. ... There was nobody to give orders. ... My position became powerless... More and more people were let in by the end of November. There were almost three thousand people crammed in by then.*

For the eight-week siege of Budapest, Lutz was holed up in his residence in the British Legation. The siege lasted till mid-February 1945. (The Pest side of the city was liberated on 18 January). The family, his staff and some Jewish children were in the basement sheltering from the barrage of bombs. They had even more reasons to be anxious than any normal target of a bombing raid—a 3,000-litre fuel tank was buried in the garden, and a well-placed bomb would blow up half the city block.

Out of 50 rooms, seven rooms remained usable, and 50 people came to seek shelter. On 25 February, the Swiss delegation crossed the river and saw at close hand the destruction from the bombs. On 22 December, the temporary government was already functioning in Debrecen, some 230 kilometres from Budapest. Delegates of the Allied Forces were already present in Debrecen. Lutz had to close the Swiss office in Budapest and take his leave. Anyone who had any relationship with the Szálasi government had to vacate Budapest.

So on 5 April 1945, Lutz handed himself over to the American and British authorities and left on 6 April. The Lutzes travelled to Istanbul via Romania where they had a few days' rest. They then boarded a ship to Lisbon and continued to Barcelona by train where the Swiss Ministry of Foreign Affairs waited to take them home. There wasn't anybody to greet him at the Swiss border when he returned—he was merely asked whether he had anything to declare.

While serving as the Swiss Vice-Consul in Budapest, from 1942 until the end of World War II, Lutz had saved thousands of Jewish lives, negotiating a deal with the Nazis and Hungarian Government to issue special Swiss safe-conduct passes to British-controlled Palestine. He boldly used his permission for 8,000 protective letters as applying to families rather than individuals, and proceeded to issue tens of thousands of additional protective letters, all of them bearing a number between one and 8,000. He also set up those 72 'safe houses' around Budapest, declaring them annexes of the Swiss legation and thus off-limits to Hungarian forces or Nazi soldiers. Among the safe houses was the 'Glass House' at 29 Vadász Street, in which up to 3,000 Hungarian Jews had found refuge.

During his time in Budapest, Carl Lutz continued to negotiate with the Hungarian and Nazi authorities, even dealing with Eichmann, as Hitler's man in Budapest, who once said, 'Lutz should be shot.'

Back in Switzerland, instead of standing ovations and recognition of his Herculean humanitarian effort, the diplomat received an official reprimand[11] for his actions in Budapest.

In addition to the official reprimand, he was met with what has been described as 'indifference, incomprehension and ill-will' rather than with the appreciation and recognition that he might have expected.

After the war, the Swiss Government subjected him to a judicial enquiry, accusing him of overstepping his 'competence'. When he was reprimanded for misuse of his authority, he was deeply wounded.

Additionally, the Soviets had arrested two diplomatic officers which led to an allegation of Nazi sympathies by the Budapest delegation.

Indeed, in 1949, when Lutz himself requested documents relating to the collective passports, he was refused and told that the Swiss Government was keeping them for 'safekeeping'. Regardless of the refusal, the investigation cleared him of wrongdoing. After the war, Lutz divorced his wife Gertrud and married his Jewish staff member, Magdalena Grausz. He adopted her young daughter Ágnes, who was then still called Ági Grausz. For the rest of his life, Carl Lutz's heroic deeds became more of a bane than a boon.

The hurt was not only emotional but also financial. In 1975, one article reported that he was considered to be in financial difficulties, much as his contemporary Oskar Schindler. For almost 50 years, Switzerland suppressed any acknowledgement of Lutz's work in Budapest. In 1995, Switzerland apologised for its decades of neglect. But for Lutz, the apology arrived 20 years too late; he had died in 1975.

Others were quicker to recognise his efforts. In 1948 he received a letter of appreciation and gratitude from the postwar Prime Minister of Hungary, Lajos Dinnyés, saying that he was 'the first amongst the diplomatic missions staff members who offered a hand to the persecuted.' The US Ambassador in Budapest wrote on 10 February 1948 that he appreciated 'the great tact, circumspection, diplomacy and personal courage' that Lutz had shown in representing America's interests. He also mentioned that Lutz was not in a position to accept the Liberty Medal. But presumably it would have been offered to him.

Perhaps most significantly for the Holocaust survivors that owe him their lives, in 1965, he was recognised by Yad Vashem (Israel's memorial to the Holocaust), which awarded Carl Lutz the title of 'Righteous Among the Nations', for his life-saving deeds.

'The scope of his actions I only recognized much later in their full dimension,' explained Agnes Hirschi, the Jewish girl Lutz adopted after the war when he married her mother, Magdalena Grausz.

Towards war's end when the Nazis were already losing the battle, they escalated their killing and persecution; Magdalena survived the end of World War II in a cellar in Budapest. For weeks, she and 40 other people who were in there did not see the light of day, and there was the danger of that 3,000-litre fuel tank in the garden exploding. To this day, Agnes Hirschi hates the darkness.

'I need the light,' said Hirschi during a later interview. She then went on to explain how it had been in January 1945, living in the bomb shelter under the burned-out building of the British Legation in the Hungarian capital. The fuel for the oil lamps and the food had gradually run out. 'Our situation was very precarious.'

In the final weeks of the war, when Budapest faced devastating air raids, no one could leave the dark basement. Gertrud Lutz, Carl's wife at the time, had taken very good care of the situation. However, survival became harder with each passing day, especially in the exceptionally cold winter of 1944-1945, when islands of ice floated on the Danube.

Hirschi remembered the hunger and fear that spread through the basement. Carl Lutz had also become increasingly nervous and thinner. Like many wartime survival stories, Hirschi considers that it was almost a miracle that she, as a seven-year-old, remained alive in that basement at war's end, in the early months of 1945.

Chapter Six
Schindler meets Kasztner

Like millions around the world, I watched *Schindler's List*, Steven Spielberg's 1993 historical epic, based on Thomas Keneally's Booker Prize-winning novel *Schindler's Ark*. The movie, a global hit winning the Academy Award for Best Picture in 1994, brought worldwide attention to the life of Oskar Schindler, and his work in Krakow.

In early 1940, Schindler set up an enamelware and munitions factory where he employed 1,000 Jews among his 1,700 workers. As World War II raged, despite having been a member of the Nazi party, he was aware of the grave danger faced by his employees as they traversed to and from their homes in the ghettos of Krakow to work in his factories. To mitigate the danger, he used all sorts of tactics to bribe and convince the German authorities that these labourers were essential workers and to allow them to continue in his factory rather than face the inevitable train ride to the death camps.

As I was researching this book on the 'good guys' in Budapest who had saved the lives of many, I started reading in more detail about Schindler. Like most of us human beings, and the heroes I set out to write about, he was not perfect. There were multiple aspects to his life that some might question. Nevertheless, he is the only 'Nazi' to be buried in the ancient Jerusalem cemetery on the Mount of Olives as a Righteous Gentile. It is his good deeds that shine through.

Steven Spielberg is a great chronicler of the human condition in all its complexity—both triumphs and foibles. He is one of my major heroes, both as a filmmaker and a recorder of Holocaust stories in the archives that he established and supported. He also might be deemed as a less than perfect human being, as he portrays his own family history in the magnificent biographical depiction of his journey as a filmmaker in the *Fablemans*. It is not our imperfections that we should be judged by, but rather what we do.

Spielberg has made amazing movies, entertaining countless millions across the globe. To my mind, his most significant achievement is the set-up of an archival system some 40 years ago so that Holocaust survivors could record their testimony, warts and all, and in their own voices. Some 59,000 survivors have recorded their testimonies to date.

Those archives have enabled me, and countless others, to hear the recorded testimony of those who experienced and survived the Holocaust. They provide a vehicle for understanding extraordinary experiences of survival, a mirror to those worlds that were not readily shared in families like mine. Neither my parents, nor Nandor, chose to share their stories, and we did not ask. The stories of others help to illuminate. As you listen to these stories, you learn in some detail of the horror, but also of individual acts of incredible humanity and courage to save others at the risk of death to themselves and their families.

So, judgement of others can be left to international courts of justice, like the Nuremberg trials, which were the most extensive in the case of the Holocaust. Or simply to readers of any book or document. My view is that as humans, we are each flawed, but nevertheless most people are weighted on the side of doing good—as best as one can—and whenever able.

Risk without glory

Some snippets of Schindler's early history highlight the life of a very colourful man. On 6 March 1928, Schindler married the daughter of a prosperous Sudeten German farmer and lived upstairs with his in-laws for seven years. Soon after marriage he quit working as a farmer, had an 18-month stint in the Czech army, and was arrested several times in 1931 and 1932 for drunkenness. Around that time had an affair with Aurelie Schlegel and had a daughter Emily, in 1933, and a son Oskar Jr, in 1935. Both were children of the affair, but Oskar later claimed the boy was not his son. Oskar's father was an alcoholic who abandoned his wife in 1935, and she died a few months later after a long illness.

Schindler was a citizen of Czechoslovakia, but considered himself to be ethnically German. In 1936, he became a spy for the Abwehr, the military intelligence service of Nazi Germany. He told Czech police when arrested that he did it for money, as by that time he had a drinking problem and was chronically in debt. He was imprisoned, then freed. In October 1938 he applied for membership of the Nazi Party.

He arrived in Krakow in October 1939 on Abwehr business. Late in 1941 he was arrested for kissing a Jewish girl, something that was not permitted under the Nuremberg Laws. A second arrest followed on 29 April 1942, again for kissing a Jewish girl on the cheek at his birthday party in the factory. In October 1944 he was again arrested for black marketeering.[1]

Following this colourful beginning, Oskar Schindler is credited with saving the lives of 1,200 of his Jewish workers by employing them. He is recognised as a humanitarian and a risk-taker. There are stories of how he saved children and others. The situation in Poland was clearly dire as populations were being sent to gas chambers. For example, 80 per cent of the Jews of Warsaw had already been murdered as had 60 per cent of those in the Lodz Ghetto, and 50 per cent of those in the Krakow Ghetto. Men and women on Schindler's 15 October 1944 list were sent to concentration camps for several weeks, but he managed to bribe authorities to release them.

Schindler travelled to Budapest on several occasions. It was felt that the Jews in neighbouring Hungary should be made aware of what was happening—the atrocities he found himself witnessing. He set up a hidden camera that captured the images of the mass graves of Polish Jews, which supposedly would have alerted the Hungarians to what was going on.

The Hungarians, as they were recording their testimonies many decades after the war were regularly asked whether they were aware of what the Germans were up to in Poland. The frequent response was that they and their families did *not know* what was happening as the freight trains took the Polish Jews to their death. In contrast, the Jewish community's leadership must have had some sense of the horrors being perpetrated across the border.

For example, Schindler himself went on a little-known clandestine journey, hiding in a newspaper van as he crossed the border and went to Budapest to meet Rezső Kasztner and others in the Jewish Relief Organisation. They trusted him enough to give him money to take to Krakow for those in labour camps, and to enlist his support to rescue 18 known activists and take them into his factory for safety. He also attempted to raise their awareness of what he so clearly saw.

Clandestine activities were risky and provided no glory. Schindler was known to be a gambler, and to be a risk-taker was perhaps a prerequisite for working in those times as a humanitarian with compassion. Historically, the main tool for humanitarians dealing with the SS was bribery. Bribery was a modus operandi for survival; Nándor Eichel used it, and Rezső Kasztner was vilified for using it with Eichmann. Schindler relied on it to prevent his workers from being executed. This went on till the end of World War II in May 1945, by which time he had spent most of his money.

As Schindler prepared to flee from the Allies, the people now remembered as the *Schindlerjuden* ('Schindler Jews') gave Schindler a gold ring made from gold fillings, engraved with the quote, **'He who saves one life saves the world entire'** from the Talmud, the book of Jewish law, that is much quoted to emphasise that saving any one life is one of the greatest human achievements.

After the war Schindler moved to West Germany and was supported by payments from Jewish relief organisations. After receiving partial reimbursement for his wartime efforts, he and his wife Emilie moved to Argentina, where they took up farming. In 1958 he went bankrupt, left his wife, and returned to Germany, where he failed in several business ventures and relied on financial support from the Schindlerjuden. He died in 1974 in Hildersheim and is buried in Jerusalem on Mount Zion.

∙∙∙

Oskar Schindler wove his survival magic in Krakow, Poland but there were many 'Schindlers' operating in Budapest—individuals beavering away and strategizing to save and rescue Jews in what was once, and again has become, beautiful Budapest. Some of these heroes appear by name and recognition in books recording the history of the times, and others may not get a line in any written manuscript. But there are witnesses, and stories to be told.

Rezső Kasztner is another flawed hero in the story. He, too, has had books written and movies made about him. A feature-length theatrical documentary, *Killing Kasztner,* was released in 2009. He has been the subject of a multi-year court case in Jerusalem. At war's end, Kasztner and his wife and daughter moved to the Jewish refugee haven of Tel Aviv. All did not go well for Kasztner, despite the records bearing witness to his attempts and success in saving many lives. But Kasztner was able to help Schindler, and without his contribution, the story of Schindler may have played out differently. Why was one man glorified, and the other vilified? History holds some clues and only some answers.

Sometimes the most helpful part of a book is the introduction—where the writer lays out the how, what, and why of their manuscript. One such book is Anna Porter's deeply researched historical biography, *Kasztner's Train: The True Story of an Unknown Hero of the Holocaust.* In the first few pages of the volume, Porter reveals some of the significant interviews of the 75 that she conducted with those who knew the man well, and who also knew Hansi Brand 'his soulmate, his lover, his partner in saving lives' without whom he claimed he could not have dealt with Eichmann.

Porter explains how she met with Egon Mayer,[2] Director of the Centre for Jewish Studies at the City University of New York, who had an archive of Kasztner information. He told Porter that his parents were on the Kasztner train, and he was born six weeks after the detachment of passengers arrived in Budapest. Porter reveals that it was Mayer who first told her that, 'it was Kasztner who had supplied the funds to feed and clothe Schindler's Jews.'

Oskar Schindler had gone to Budapest in 1942 to meet Kasztner. They were two very different men. Each of the men had powerful egos, believing they could outwit the Nazis. In other ways the two men were very different: the 'large-boned rough-talking' German-speaking Schindler and the softly spoken, intellectual Hungarian Kasztner. Of course, there were lesser aspects of his personality as described by his detractors.

Initially the two men had not liked each other, but with subsequent meetings, exchanging letters, cash, and information in the common cause of saving Jews, Schindler 'learned to admire' Kasztner. 'He was utterly fearless' and in a postwar memoir he wrote, 'His actions remain unsurpassed.'

And as Porter notes, one man is lionised and the other is considered a symbol of German collaboration with the enemy. The question could be asked, how far should a person go to save the lives of others?[3]

The journalist who saw it coming

On 12 March 1938, Germany occupied Austria. Over 500 Jews committed suicide during the first weeks of the 'Anschluss', the term by which the annexation of Austria was known. Within a year, 100,000 Austrian Jews emigrated to, for example, Palestine, the United States or Hungary.

Late in the 1930s, in Nuremberg, a new exhibition opened under the title, *The External Jew*. It denounced Jews as a disease, a virus that infected Aryan races, and equated Judaism to Bolshevism. A film of the same title, featuring Jews as plague-carrying rats, went into production.

In September 1938, when Hitler gained Czechoslovakia by convincing British, French and Italian leaders of Germany's right to the Sudetenland part of Czechoslovakia, the many German and Austrian Jews who'd taken refuge in Slovakia were displaced again.

On 9 November 1938, the terror of Kristallnacht or *Night of the Broken Glass* took place and 191 Synagogues were burned or destroyed with axes and hammers—shops looted, tombstones were uprooted, homes smashed, and Jews found in the streets were beaten throughout Germany. That is when many, like one of my uncles, who later married my father's sister in Israel after the war, knew that it was time to leave Germany. He went to Israel as fast as he could.

Meanwhile in Budapest, many Hungarian Jews watched nervously, as they were still able to read newspapers, listen to the radio and receive first-hand reports from travellers. My own father could have been on one of his many trips to Vienna or Berlin to make a deal for the onions and garlic that he traded in Europe. The Jews considered that Hungary would be safe from the Nazi genocide. Indeed, as Eastern European cities were annexed and put under antisemitic codes of law, Budapest was seen as one of the few safe havens for Jewish refugees. Not everyone was convinced.

It was at that time in 1938 when Rezső, (also known as Rudolf), Kasztner was still a lawyer and a journalist on the Hungarian language newspaper *Új Kelet* in Kolozsvár, predicted that Hitler would be coming for the 500,000 German-speaking Jews.

Új Kelet as newspaper was a significant player in Kasztner's life and also in the life of the pre-war and post-war Hungarian communities around the world, like my family in Australia.

Refugees from Poland, Slovakia, Austria, and other countries poured into Hungary and Romania. Kasztner, despite government orders forbidding aid to refugees, set up an information centre in Kolozsvár for those seeking accommodation, clothing, and food, but also for those looking for a safe destination.

When Paris fell to the Nazis on 14 June 1940, Kasztner mourned the passing of an age. He wrote in *Uj Kelet*, ' ... a page has turned in the history of France, Europe and humanity at large'. He saw France as the bastion of 'common sense, freedom and democracy' and the victory of a regime that 'negates' these values was a turning point in history.

When it came to Hungary, for Kasztner and the wider leadership of Hungary, Ferenc Szálasi was considered to be a fringe figure in the 1930s, making racist diatribes, inciting vandalism against Jews, and he practised spiritualism with the Bible being written in some early form of Hungarian, and even claimed that Jesus was Magyar.[4]

When his Arrow Cross, otherwise known as the *Nyilas,* threw hand grenades into Dohány Street Synagogue, the perpetrators received light sentences. The party became illegal in February 1938, but subsequently, towards war's end, the party and the Arrow Cross apparatchiks were the feared tyrants, and today they can be described more accurately as 'terrorists' who had an extraordinary reign of terror in Hungary, particularly in Budapest, over a relatively short period of time.

By early 1941, the Hungarian government had already closed all Jewish newspapers, including *Uj Kelet.* Kasztner went to Budapest where the economy seemed to be booming. Theatres were playing Shakespeare, and Váci Street was the grand boulevard where well-groomed shoppers were promenading. The opera season was in full swing with *Faust, Cosi fan Tutte* and *The Marriage of Figaro* showing, and the 'worst restaurants offered better food than the best restaurants in Kolozsvár'.

The magnificent parliament building boasted that it was the largest in the world when it opened in 1902. At the Comedy Theatre they were laughing at Hitler. There were nightclubs, opera and cafes and casinos. At night, 'Pest lit up like a Christmas tree'. Budapest was cosmopolitan. This is the Budapest that my family knew and loved. The majority of the city's residents were not yet aware of the impending disaster that was to come their way a mere three years later.

Kasztner comes to Budapest

In Budapest, Kasztner rented a small two-room flat in a pension in the grand Váci Street near Vörösmarty and the Gerbaud restaurant. To this day, Gerbaud offers the most tantalising of Hungarian cakes, like Dobos. The Dobos parfait, as we learnt in 2023, is any sweet lover's dream, albeit an excess. The pension's owner, Elizabeth Zahler, played the piano and sang popular love songs. She was a divorcee with a teenage daughter. Rezső and she spent time together until late July 1941, when Bogyó (his wife) arrived in Budapest.

Kasztner had an introduction from his father-in-law, József Fisher, to Ottó Komoly, the President of the Budapest Zionist Association, and Komoly encouraged him to seek out Miklós Moshe Krausz, the Jewish Agency's man in Budapest. The Palestine office was at that time on Erzsebet Boulevard. Kasztner was working on the Va'ada, the Aid and Rescue Committee. He set about arranging Palestine visas for the refugees.

The Palestine office was a crowded place of chaos and desperation, with people seeking entry to a place of refuge like Palestine which required a British certificate. Kasztner was not one to wait in a queue. He barged in and saw Moshe Krausz, 'a thin, bespectacled, middle-aged man with an unusually large head balanced on a long neck that popped up from behind the desk'. Krausz was outraged at the interruption. Kasztner was interested in his refugees, and Krausz was interested in sticking to rules with the British and Palestine immigration offices. There were more than 100 refugees on the stairs and more in the waiting rooms. Krausz didn't like the forceful, loud, insistent Kasztner. He was unlike the modest, quietly spoken heroes like Lutz, Eichel and Wallenberg's assistant, Farkas. More about him later.

Already in 1941, Kasztner urged Krausz to include families in the certificates. But Krausz was one to stick to the rules and not ruffle the feathers of the British. In later years, there was a great deal made of those certificates that saved so many lives when Carl Lutz, acting in the role of the Swiss ambassador and Raoul Wallenberg, the Swedish ambassador, were credited with devising the 'ingenious' method of including a whole family as an individual on what were later known as Schutzpasse and issuing them to their respective countries.

There has been conjecture that if this system had been introduced earlier, it's possible many lives could have been saved. But then would the Hungarian authorities have agreed, as they later did? Krausz steadfastly insisted on sticking to the rules, and Kasztner despised Krausz for it. However, he was not the only one that Kasztner bristled against in his humanitarian work.

Samu Stern, Head of the National Bureau of Hungarian Jewry at 12 Síp Street, was another man who was not sympathetic to Kasztner.

Kasztner was introduced to Joel Brand and his wife, Hansi Brand, who was helping refugees by running a glove factory for them. In fact, their apartment was the first port of call for refugees. Brand found Kasztner intense; an overbearing man who liked to dominate a conversation, restless, impatient, barely listening. Kasztner spent a lot of time with Joel's wife, Hansi. The Brands were not considered to have a happy marriage, but one described as a marriage of convenience.

Great Britain declared war on Hungary on 7 December 1941, and Hitler declared war on the US on 11 December. In December, Oskar Schindler travelled on that freight car filled with Nazi Party newspapers. Springman and Kasztner met him at the Hotel Pannonia in Pest. Schindler talked about the atrocities of Krakow, describing trainloads of Jews leaving Warsaw for extermination camps.

Kasztner did not feel comfortable in the presence of Schindler, who he thought ' ... was still enriching himself by slave labour'.[5]

Under Miklós Kállay, Prime Minister of Hungary since March 1942, industries were surviving. Kállay was resisting bringing in any further anti-Jewish laws and gave credence to Stern's theory that 'It cannot happen here.'

The ghetto rebellion in Warsaw, April–May 1943, was not reported on Budapest radio. News of war was generally gathered through BBC broadcasts.

In the summer of 1943, Oskar Schindler returned for a second visit to Budapest. Kasztner urged him to increase the number of workers in a protected Jewish camp near his factory, and he was able to replenish the funds that Schindler had advanced to hire workers.

Kasztner had already heard of the gas chambers that had by then consumed half a million people, but at first disbelieved that it could happen. He was subsequently judged for not making the facts of this devastation better known.

Others had raised awareness in any way they could, sometimes by the extreme action of suicide. For example, before he committed suicide in London, Samuel Zygelbojm, a former leader of the Jewish Socialist Party in Poland and a member of the Polish government in exile, wrote a letter:

> *With these my last words ... of the three and a half million Polish Jews (to whom must be added the 700,000 deported from other countries) in April 1943 there remained alive not more than three hundred thousand ... and the extermination continues. I cannot remain silent ... let my death be an energetic cry of protest against the indifference of the world ...*[6]

When the Germans came to town

On 4 October 1943, one day before I was born, at a meeting of SS generals in Poznan, Heinrich Himmler boasted that only his SS could have carried out the 'action' against the Jews. 'This steadfast killing spree' he said, was 'a page of glory in its history which could never be truly appreciated.'

Himmler spoke for several hours at this meeting, and the transcript of his chilling speech extends for 116 pages. It generally displays the depravity of his extermination mindset. There was a core of Nazi leadership that had absorbed Hitler's antisemitism and was willing to put it into action.

The fury of the war reached Budapest on 19 March 1944, as the German army occupied Hungary; the tanks rolled into Andrássy út, the grand boulevard. By 9 am, most of Budapest knew that Germans had invaded, and that was not from Radio Budapest which played light music as if nothing had happened. There were no newspapers and only the BBC announced the occupation. The Government of Miklós Kállay dissolved; the Prime Minister had fled to the Turkish legation and begged for asylum.

In 2023 I walk down Andrássy út, the Champs Élysées of Budapest, the most beautiful and prestigious avenue in Hungary. As one passes the Opera House, the Liszt Ferenc Music Academy and elegant high-street shops, there are echoes of the rich Jewish cultural legacy of Budapest.

But for the Jewish history that I came to revisit in my mind's eye, I hear the descriptions of those who were looking down from their comfortable apartments above those shops as the German tanks rolled in on 19 March 1944. As one survivor described it, it was 'the end of my childhood' and the start of a period of unforgettable dread until the day of liberation.

It was on 27 March that Kasztner had gone in a distressed state at dawn to see Carl Lutz, the Swiss consul who was already located in the American Embassy in Szabadság Square. The Swiss represented US interests in Hungary.

On 31 March, Eichmann summoned the Central Jewish Council to his office at the Majestic Hotel and the adjunct Little Majestic. On the way up Swabian Hill the men were stopped on several occasions and asked for identification. The buildings were surrounded by three rings of barbed wire fencing. There were guard dogs surrounding the periphery. The men walked through corridors. They were searched and checked, then they walked through a second set of heavy wooden doors before reaching another SS man and being subjected to a second search.[7]

Eichmann's office was on the second floor and Baky's office, (one of the Hungarian government's two political State Secretaries) was on the third floor. Eichmann shouted, 'I am a bloodhound!' Those who resisted would be shot. He wanted workers, and demanded that the yellow stars had to be made by 5 pm that day, when they had to be worn.

When he was told it was not possible, he relented and said that temporary stars could be used for the first two days. He demanded 400 workers. The temporary star is meaningfully on display at the Memorial Museum of Hungarian Speaking Jewry in Safed, Israel. There was no time to monogram anything on the star.

That same day, new laws were enacted that stated that Jews could not employ non-Jews; could not work as lawyers, journalists, be a public servant or work in the theatre, film or arts; they were not allowed to own vehicles or drive motorbikes or bicycles. They had to hand in radios or telephones to central authorities in charge of Jewish affairs, and if not surrender, would be arrested—plus they had to wear yellow stars for 'differentiation'.

The next day, the government banned all Hungarians from listening to foreign radio stations. The antisemitic film, *The Jew Suss (Jud Suss)* was playing to packed houses in cinemas.

Newspapers ran stories of *The Protocols of the Elders of Zion*, a highly influential work of antisemitism originating in Russia shortly before World War I. It is a fabricated text put together from various sources that describes a plot by Jews for global domination. It was translated into multiple languages and assigned from 1938 by some teachers in Nazi Germany as factual material to be read by schoolchildren. Although the text had been exposed as fraudulent already in 1921 and 1924, it continued, and continues, as a most influential work of antisemitism.

On 25 June 1944:

> *... the primate of the Church of England, William Temple, denounced the deportations, and Francis Cardinal Spellman in the United States called on Roman Catholics to rise up against the evil of racial persecution.*

Both messages were carried by the BBC and widely heard in Budapest, despite the prohibition of listening to enemy broadcasts.

> 'The American press threatened the Hungarian society, as a whole, and Regent Miklós Horthy, personally, would be judged guilty of complicity. King Gustav V of Sweden sent an urgent appeal to Horthy ... Max Huber, the president of the International Red Cross, wrote to Horthy ...' Huber offered to send a mission to Hungary with food and clothing for deportees.[8]

And there were others, but it all did not seem to help when it came to deportations and death.

By the end of June, more than 400,000 people were deported to Auschwitz.

Bartering for lives; blood for goods

Meanwhile that afternoon of the 25th June, 1944, the Va'ada,[9] The Aid and Rescue Committee which included Kasztner as a member, met at the Café Parisette in Vörösmarty Square not far from the Duna Corso waterfront. Sunday strollers, not having their freedoms curtailed, despite the seriousness of the impending disaster to be experienced by the whole community, may have been enjoying the sunshine, as do the tourists in 2023. According to Komoly, President of the Aid and Rescue Committee, the priority was to assist the Jews with 'unsettled citizenship'.

It was the suggestion of Hansi Brand that they employ a strategy used by the Bratislava Working Group Europa's plan to 'negotiate to buy lives' and Kasztner agreed. At that point, no one returned to their homes—it was too dangerous—Kasztner and the Brands all went to a more gentile neighbourhood that was a distance from the centre of Budapest. The Palestine Office was already closed. Krausz had vanished.

Döme Sztójay was named Prime Minister. László Baky, one of two political State Secretaries picked by Sztójay, had served in the Hungarian military and gendarmerie, and had retired to devote himself to politics. He had belonged to the Arrow Cross Party in 1938 but switched to the Hungarian Nationalist

Socialist Party and its newspaper *Magyarság (Hungarianness)* known for his diatribes against the Jews.

Hungarian radio reported that Jews could no longer emigrate. It was Kasztner who reportedly said that this would not apply if the Jews were citizens of another country. Thus, the answer according to Kasztner was to *make* Jews citizens of another country. Lutz said he would follow up with the Hungarian authorities. So it seems that Kasztner may have given Lutz the good idea about citizenship and passes, and Lutz made it happen.

Kasztner and Brand went to the Majestic Hotel to deliver the cash. There was an expectation that payments of money would stop deportations. There was talk of a payment of US$3 million to stop all deportations, (equivalent to $25 million US dollars in 2025). They could only raise three million pengős (approximately $600,000) since the money was not coming from the American JDC.

Hermann Krumey, the head SS man in charge of Eichmann's Sonderkommando in Budapest, agreed they could take 600 emigrants (half from regions) and could take another 300 for 100,000 additional pengős, which he considered to be a paltry sum as he had been offered much more. Also there was current hyperinflation and the pengő was not worth much, just 20 cents at the time, and on the black market the value of the dollar was as low as 11-13 cents.

There was urgency to act. In the first week of May, 1944, the Kolozsvár ghetto was established at the old brickworks, with a roof but no real walls, and practically no facilities. It was where 18,000 Jews were assembled at the northern part of the city and surrounds. It was the city where Kasztner's family and extended family were. His father-in-law József Fischer was head of the Jewish Council that oversaw the internal administration. Between 25 May and 9 June, six transports with 16,148 inhabitants left from that location to Auschwitz, some 75 per cent of those people were sent to the gas chambers. Some 1,000 Jewish survivors returned to the city at war's end when it was renamed Cluj (and more recently Cluj-Napoca). Ernő Márton, one of the members of the Jewish leadership in the ghetto and the former editor of *Új Kelet* (who would later work again with Kasztner at the reopening of the newspaper in Israel), managed to escape Kolozsvár, through Romania to Israel.

Kasztner visited Kolozsvár between 4 and 5 May and arranged to have 388 Jews from the notorious ghetto released to a special camp in Budapest, the Columbus Street camp.

The bargaining between Eichmann and Kasztner was known as 'Blood for Goods' 10,000 trucks for one million lives, that is, one truck for every 100 lives. On 28 April Eichmann summoned Brand back to the Majestic Hotel and said he now had consent to continue the discussions for the 10,000 trucks. Brand wanted all the Jews. One million is all that Eichmann was prepared to discuss, and 10,000 trucks.

There was also bargaining for apartments. When the Swiss Ambassador was asked to produce 500 apartments, it then increased to 1,500.

Carl Lutz asked the Hungarian government to allow those with Palestinian certificates to leave immediately. Lutz handed out Swiss immigration papers. The number at the top was always under 700. He hired clerks from Slovak, Polish and Hungarian young Zionist youth who had sought refuge at the Embassy as workers to help.

The atmosphere was fraught. Hansi Brand and Kasztner were bargaining with Eichmann whilst Hansi's husband was in Istanbul, negotiating with the authorities to gain entry into British-controlled Palestine and to obtain trucks in return for safe passage. The Jewish authorities were always suspicious of supporting the German war effort with trucks and money.

Meanwhile, the transports continued.

Whilst Hansi Brand's husband Joel was in Istanbul negotiating with the officials representing the British Mandate in Palestine, on 19 May, she was summoned by Eichmann to the Majestic Hotel. Eichmann was wondering what her husband was up to and threateningly told her that, 'He is on thin ice'.

There was an irony in Eichmann's choice of words as the lives of 30,000 people were considered to be 'on ice' whilst waiting for word from Istanbul. At that stage, there was still some hope and expectation that the rescue and transportation to freedom could be achieved for the 30,000 through negotiations and bargaining.

During the first two days that Brand was away, 23,363 Hungarians were deported; by 19 May the number had increased to 62,644.

Kasztner begged for the deportation to stop. Eichmann said he would not stop the trains. Finally, Lutz got the Swiss Ambassador's support to send the *Auschwitz Protocols* to Berne as long as the Nazis could not find any connection to the Swiss Consulate. Krausz had already sent them.

The next meeting that Kasztner had with Eichmann was on 22 May. This time he took his own cigarettes as he had not been offered a drink or cigars at previous meetings. Eichmann, wearing his jackboots, strutted up and down shouting obscenities.

Kasztner gave him a list of 600 Jewish families. The group would have to travel through Germany, France, Spain and then onto Africa. Permission needed to be obtained from these countries for safe passage.

Bunkers were being dug as bombings were expected. Trains were leaving for the extermination camp, four a day, seven days a week. The next target was the Jews of Zone IV South-Eastern Hungary, which included Szeged, only 50 kilometres from Makó where my father's family, the Strausz's, were rounded up.

Kurt Andreus Becher was Himmler's man in Budapest. He was 34 years old, tall, and good-looking. He had successfully negotiated to have the rights to the assets of the Chorin-Weiss-Kornfeld-Mauthner family, including aircraft and munitions, in return for the Chorin group's safe passage to a neutral country: Spain, or Portugal. They had already left on 18 May. Kasztner wanted a new negotiation partner, and that turned out to be Becher, whose record of successful negotiations was very attractive to him.

Kasztner showed Eichmann the *Auschwitz Protocols* to which he replied, 'You don't believe all this. ' On 16 June, Hansi and Kasztner were summoned to the Majestic Hotel.

On 10 June, a train with 388 passengers left Kolozsvár. The passengers arrived at Columbus Street in Budapest, beaten and dressed in rags. A hospital was set up to look after them. The people were housed at the Wechselmann Institute where Kasztner and Hansi had their offices. At this point, Kasztner's wife, Bogyó, also moved in.

On 30 June 1944, Kasztner's group of 1,684 Jews left the Columbus Street group camp in Budapest from Rákos Street railway station and eventually reached Switzerland via Bergen-Belsen. These have been described as a group representing a 'token of SS goodwill' in negotiations with the Allies. Kasztner's goal had been to save the remaining Jews of Budapest, numbering in the hundreds of thousands.[10]

There were 150 places for those who could pay with money or jewels. There were 40 Rabbis, including the fabled Szatmár Rabbi of the ultrareligious Chassidim, who also provided testimony in Kasztner's trial in Israel some years later. There were opera singers, scholars, journalists, landowners, peasants, and former officers in the Hungarian army, Polish and Hungarian orphans. There were Joel Brand's mother and sister, and some of Kasztner's and his wife Bogyó's family, along with the families of the Jewish communal leaders like Samu Stern and Ottó Komoly. It was described as a 'kind of Noah's Ark'.[11]

It was far from smooth sailing from hereon. Kasztner himself was arrested on 15 July by the Hungarian police and interrogated for six days.

In one of Rezső Kasztner's own publications, there is a poignant reference to '*A nagy embervásár...*' translated as, *The Great Human Fair*: the bartering for lives when there are trade-offs or exchanges of humans for trucks and money. Bartering for one commodity or another is not an uncommon feature in wartime hostage negotiations. Kasztner summed up the times:

To anyone who was not there, most of these events will seem to be incomprehensible, paradoxical, unbelievable. We lived in insane times. Even to us, everything that happened remains impossible to grasp. In those times the human mind could not apply normal rules of logic.[12]

Kasztner's well-chosen words reflect the extraordinary risks that some humans take to effect the rescue of others. It was not only Kasztner[13] who paid the ultimate price for his efforts. He was one man who would have wanted the accolades and did not get them, but there were also others who did.

Chapter Seven
Raoul Wallenberg: Another Budapesti Schindler

Raoul Wallenberg, the Swedish diplomat in Budapest in 1944, has also been credited with saving many thousands of Jews during the last stages of the war there. In many ways he is recognised as a hero and a 'legend' with a well-recognised name. He has been honoured in numerous countries with statues and memorial days, acknowledging his work to save Hungarian Jewry.

The fact that mystery has shrouded his fate and disappearance for decades has added to his renown by those who study this period of history. Unlike Carl Lutz, Wallenberg was born into a distinguished Swedish banking and diplomatic family and went to Budapest under Swedish diplomatic cover. A converted Lutheran, he was the great-great-grandson of one of the first Jews who had settled in Sweden. His family controlled Stockholm's Enskilda Bank, a financial institution that continued to deal with both the Allies and the Axis. Both he and Lutz had spent time in the United States where they studied, and in Israel, where Wallenberg spent six months in Haifa. There he studied management at the Holland Bank, and it was there that he first met with Jewish refugees from Germany. When he returned to Stockholm he became the foreign representative of a central European trading company, whose president was a Hungarian Jew, Kálmán Lauer.

By May 1944 the credible accounts of what was happening in the extermination camps finally reached the Western world. It came from Rudolf Vrba and Alfréd Wetzler, the two Jews who had managed to escape the gas chambers and Nazi Germany. By then the Jews of Budapest feared what was to come. That is when they asked the embassies of neutral countries for help with provisional identity passes.

The American War Refugee Board was set up to assist. The Swiss Legation and Carl Lutz were already in Budapest.

It was not until July 1944, at the request of the Hungarian Jewish leadership, that Wallenberg was sent on a diplomatic mission to Hungary as an attaché of the Swedish Embassy. By that time, between 437,000 and 440,000 Jews had already been deported to extermination camps, mainly from the provinces, and in Budapest, a quarter million Jews were wearing the yellow star. After March 1944, the Allies saw what was happening. The newly established US War Refugee Board (WRB) asked neutral countries to send emissaries/observers. Wallenberg volunteered. Although some considered him too young and inexperienced, his Hungarian business partner, Kalman Lauer, was persistent in his belief that Wallenberg was the right man for the job in Budapest: a quick thinker, energetic, brave, and compassionate. And he had come from a famous Swedish banking family.

He was specifically sent to save Jews. The position was funded by the WRB, the American JDC and the Swedish Government. Before accepting the post he had clear requirements that included access to large sums of money for purposes of buying favour or goods, and he did not want to be restrained by bureaucratic protocols. He requested diplomatic status, freedom to approach any group in Hungary, and freedom from restrictions that limited him from only working with conventional diplomatic channels. Initially he was credited as a Third Secretary to the Swedish Embassy in Hungary.

He arrived in Budapest on 9th July, 1944, three days too late to see the last train for Auschwitz leave outer Budapest suburbs. Perhaps his distress on discovering that would have contributed to his resolve to make up for lost time.

The hundredth birthday celebrations

In Sydney, Australia, on 5 September 2012, at a celebration of what would have been Raoul Wallenberg's 100th birthday, there were amazing stories of survival and achievement.

Ervin Forrester told the gathering that day that he had a life-saving brush with Wallenberg in December 1944 when he was moved with a group of Hungarian Jews from Budapest to Sopron, a town near the Austrian border. He went on to say:

> We were placed in homes in the village and used as slave labour. All the others were eventually moved to Mauthausen (A concentration camp in Austria) but I escaped. I tried to buy a rail ticket back to Budapest, but the Russians had bombed the tracks. The only way I could get back was to trick Germans into believing I was a member of the Hitler Youth as I was wearing an armband stating that I was a military worker. A Wehrmacht officer believed my story and drove me back to Budapest. I had to find somewhere to stay and was put up by the Red Cross. But one day, the Hungarian Nazis surrounded the building in which about 20 of us were staying and we were arrested. I was charged by a military court of desertion and sentenced to death.

The 20-year-old had only one chance of survival, as he told it:

> I told the court that I was a Swedish citizen and on that basis, they could not detain me. They sent all my details to Wallenberg who did not know me but who understood what was going on. Wallenberg was at the jail within an hour with the necessary papers and I was freed and spent the rest of the war under Swedish protection.

Wallenberg's efforts to save lives were numerous and often ingenious. His chief operation was the distribution of the Swedish certificates of protection, also known as Wallenberg Passports, or Schutzpasses, which were initially granted to those who had some link with Sweden, but which were much the same as those granted by the Swiss Carl Lutz. He, too, was credited with applying pressure to the Hungarian Government. His department, 'Section 3—for Humanitarian Aims', employed 400 Jews. When the Arrow Cross came to power, Wallenberg is also credited with initiating the 'international ghetto.' This meant improvising a series of safe houses for refuge, by flying the flags of neutral countries like Switzerland, Sweden, Spain, Portugal and the Vatican mission. Together, these protected about 33,000 Jews, 7,000 of whom had Swedish protection.

He managed to free some 500 persons and return them to Budapest. He saved several hundred labour detachments that had been put on the deportation train. In Budapest, he organised a 'Jewish Guard' consisting of Aryan-looking Jews dressed in SS and Arrow Cross uniforms, and established hospitals and soup kitchens.

He was another one that Eichmann threatened to kill, referring to him as 'Judenhund Wallenberg.'

When it was no longer possible to transport the Jews by train, the death marches to the Austrian border began.

As war neared its end in November 1944, thousands of Budapest Jews, men, women and children, were forced on a 'death march' via the town of Hegyeshalom, to the Austrian border as an agreed labour force of able-bodied persons. Images of those roundups show men and women with hands aloft looking straight ahead while the Nyilas must have been threatening on the sidelines with their guns and bayonets at the ready. Wallenberg and the Embassy secretary, Per Anger, followed them with a convoy of trucks carrying food and clothing. Wallenberg himself distributed medicines to the dying, and food and clothing to the marchers, as well as Swedish passes to win their freedom if they could escape.

Ultimately, Wallenberg's heroism did not save him. Mid-January 1945, the Russians marched in. He was questioned by the Soviets on suspicion of espionage, arrested, and was reported as having died in 1953 in the Lubyanka prison. Rumours abound that the Soviets executed him.

Who gets credit for what?

What does it really matter who did what, when? Does it matter who gets the credit for what happens in the chaos of war if lives are saved? Who writes the history when there are no eyewitnesses and personal recordings of events? Perhaps there is more than one version of events.

These are the questions that come to mind when I read of the activities of Carl Lutz and Raoul Wallenberg, the Swiss and Swedish diplomats in Hungary in the turbulent year of 1944–1945. In the turmoil of war, one can generally assume that good people were collecting good ideas, whether they be their own or those of others, and working to action them.

In this case, their unique brand of heroism required Hungarian government authorisation which has been verified through access to cabinet documents. The two key diplomats representing the neutral powers swiftly took action. They used their diplomacy and skills in working both independently and together to approach, influence, or otherwise win over authorities. In this way, they were able to make things happen for others.

It was in Anna Porter's book that I first read that Rezső Kasztner had suggested to the clerically-minded Moshe Krausz that groups rather than individuals be named on exit certificates, to maximise the use of limited quotas that were available for refugees. Other sources imply that it was Per Anger, who worked with Raoul Wallenberg in the Swedish Embassy, who had the good idea of the passes. Or was it the Swiss consul, Carl Lutz? Different sources claim different points of genesis for the idea. Whoever it was, both Lutz and Wallenberg are acknowledged as using their position and influence and risking their own lives to save others.

Biographers tend to ascribe maximum credit to each of their heroes. Randolph Braham—that most detailed historian of the period—writes on page 964 in the second volume of his historical masterpiece of those times, that: 'Wallenberg and Lutz paid frequent visits to the brickyards to reclaim their wards and to distribute protective passes. Additionally, many were smuggled out by young youth workers wearing SS or Arrow Cross uniforms. And then there were those saved by being provided Christian identification papers, often with the cooperation of sympathetic police officers.'

Good people operate in the most dire of circumstances, and credit can never be meted out in equal measure.

•••

Wallenberg is widely recognised as a hero, lauded for the risks he took on behalf of the defenceless. However, on the record, here and there, moments of flawed humanity shine through the generally hagiographic histories. Take the firsthand account of Andor Schwartz, who met him once at the Glass House when he came to meet Lutz and Krausz:

> 'As a porter in Vadász Street I personally met Raoul Wallenberg only once. He came just for a few minutes and went as quickly as possible. At his side was a striking looking Jewish girl. She was, in my opinion, some motivation for him to help, but don't take any notice of my opinion. He was a hero and sometimes his life was in the same danger as those he protected. He definitely saved thousands and thousands of Jewish lives.'

It's a truism that heroism is defined by actions, not intentions. There are memorials to Wallenberg all over the world—in Budapest, Tel Aviv, London, Argentina, the United States and here in Australia, in Melbourne, where I live.

He is an embodiment of the Jewish proverb reminding us that even when we are without choice, we can mobilise the spirit of courage. Raoul Wallenberg's fate may never be known for sure. He has no grave. But his legacy endures.

The thrill of a find

When one embarks upon a research journey it is a bit like being a detective, and there is always the thrill of the find. One such highlight was my meeting with Frank Vajda, the well-respected, well-published neurologist, at the University of Melbourne, whose book, *Saved to Remember: Raoul Wallenberg, Budapest 1944 and After* was published by Monash University Press in 2016.

Frank had researched and written about that period for the previous 40 years. Since the day in 1982 when he first heard a promotion for a documentary on Raoul Wallenberg, Vajda's research, writing, public speaking and actions about Wallenberg changed his life.

The promotional advertisement described how this man would jump onto the back of a cattle truck and call out names of people who were recorded on the Schutzpasses, those certificates claiming them to be citizens of Sweden and thus under Swedish protection, whilst bullets were being shot over his head.

Those on the list were saved from the last transport to Auschwitz. In this promotion, Frank heard the echo of his own family story and began to devote himself to Wallenberg's legacy. For decades, he fought to create the recognition and appreciation of Wallenberg's feats of rescue.

Whilst he, like many others, was not able to solve the mystery of Wallenberg's postwar disappearance and death, he did manage to have Wallenberg recognised as an honorary citizen of Australia, as had the US, Canada and Israel all recognised him as their honorary citizen. Vajda also managed to achieve the acquisition of a magnificent bust of Wallenberg, made by Polish-born Viennese–Australian sculptor Karl Duldig, which now stands in clear view near a busy junction in the beautiful leafy suburb of Kew in Melbourne, Australia.

As part of his life's historical work, Frank translated Jenő Lévai's, (also published in English as Eugene) Hungarian book: *Raoul Wallenberg*, written in 1946; a book that made its way to me. Lévai was a renowned journalist and documenter of the era.

It was a true find. I would have liked to reprint much of it in its entirety. The book contains the details of Wallenberg's reports to Sweden on what he found when he went to Budapest. He wrote his first report on 17 July, eight days after his arrival.

It was a detailed description of the internments, the ghettos, the death marches, from which Wallenberg and Per Anger were the two diplomatic representatives able to rescue people with their 'Swedish documents'. The book details the *Auschwitz Documents* which describe the horrors and the preparation of mass graves in the concentration camps of Poland, the mass killings, gassing and cremation of humans by the thousands in the ovens of Auschwitz.[1]

Then there are the activities of the Arrow Cross on Christmas Day 1944, when they conducted raids on children's homes, where children and their adult carers were shot at point-blank range. There are accounts of that time when Wallenberg carried all his possessions in a knapsack and spent each night in a different place for his own safety.

Lévai's book contains a lengthy discussion about Wallenberg's personality and how he was a 'great rescuer'. He was described as 'impulsive with a tendency to pessimism'. There were numerous instances when even the dead-tired Wallenberg tended to lose heart. His collaborators knew him well, however. At these times, a good joke, or a witty saying, but more particularly some *result*, even if on rather a small scale—such as saving a single person—immediately altered his dark mood and once again he became the enthusiastic leader.[2]

He managed impressive operations with some bravado. He carried off difficult stunts—and the more daring, the more dangerous they were, the greater the motivator for him to try something *more* adventurous and dangerous the next time. He was not born a death-defying hero. He was self-deprecating and described himself as 'Hasenfuss'—a timid rabbit. He was daring in the defence of others and seems to have overcome his personality limitations.

By the time Wallenberg arrived in Budapest in July 1944, the Germans, under the leadership of SS Officer Adolf Eichmann, had already deported between 400,000 and 437,000 Jewish men, women and children mainly from the provinces in Hungary. They had been transported on 148 freight trains between 14 May and 8 July. Only about 230,000–255,000 Jews were now left, out of a population that in 1941 had numbered close to 825,000.

When in October 1944 Jews were being loaded into cattle trucks to be sent to Auschwitz, Wallenberg systematically designed, printed, and organised the issue of those Swedish protective passports. He and his aids would go to the railway stations and hand the passports that would automatically give the recipient protection as citizens of a neutral country.

Within the 1,400+ pages of the work of the preeminent historian of the period, Randolph Braham, (who is not often found to be moved to hyperbole), he describes Wallenberg's work in Budapest as being of 'heroic' proportions, particularly during the period of the siege of Budapest by the Red Army. At that time, the capital was in a state of anarchy, and the Nyilas were roaming the streets of the city, venting their frustration on the Jews. He struggled to save them from the Nyilas and strove to supply food for the tens of thousands of Jews in the ghetto and protected buildings. By then the regular sources of food supplies were difficult to come by.

Both the Nazis and the Hungarian Nyilas were planning to destroy the ghetto. And as Braham points out, in the midst of the chaos and rescues, he managed to file his reports about the specifics and the magnitude of the catastrophe.[3]

Eichmann departed Budapest on 24 December. Before he left, he issued orders to raze the ghetto and machine-gun the inhabitants. The order was ready—execution squads were ready to go into action—when Wallenberg saved the ghetto by sending a message to the commanding SS General, charging him with criminal responsibility if he carried out the order, whilst threatening to testify against him after the war.

The Nazi cancelled the action.

This act alone is said to have saved 80,000 Jews.

Jenő Lévai's book describes in detail this planned mass murder, naming the principal German and Hungarian units involved and their criminal commanders who were about to embark on the machine-gunning of the inhabitants within a few hours. The book claims that virtually all who survived in Budapest owe their lives to Wallenberg. But of course, there were many others who are owed such credit.

Lévai's book reports that Wallenberg and Per Anger were the only two foreign diplomats who personally went along the death marches to Hegyeshalom in order to rescue the Jews. Wallenberg organised trucks to Red Cross, Swedish, Swiss and Portuguese Legations.[4]

One could write an almost parallel heroic statement about Carl Lutz—he too is credited for saving most of those 200,000 Jews, so the likelihood is that they all worked very closely together in the ambassadorial environment.

Which brings me back to my central preoccupation—the big question, binding all the other questions for which I'm seeking answers: the question of silence.

Wallenberg's fate ends in silence and sadness, behind the hush of the Iron Curtain, but his actions are recalled forever through deed, document, and the memory of those he saved.

But who worked alongside him? None of the Budapesti Schindlers worked in isolation. The salvation of the Jews of Budapest, who lived beyond the Holocaust, was a concerted effort, with many actors each playing their part.

How many other heroes were there in Budapest—that last domino to fall in the Holocaust—who, for their own reasons, never spoke of their actions?

I know of at least one or two.

Farkas—The man with Wallenberg

One reason for Frank Vadja's devotion to the legacy of Wallenberg is highly personal, as Wallenberg saved Vadja's life when he was a nine-year-old in Budapest. He and his family had been reported to the authorities for not wearing the yellow Star of David that was compulsory for Jews to wear in public. A band of armed men came and seized them and dragged them to a military barracks where they were lined up in front of a machine gun. The soldiers were debating whether to shoot them on the spot or throw them into the Danube when some men in civilian clothing suddenly appeared—Raoul Wallenberg, accompanied by his escort, negotiated their safe release.

The escort was most likely a man named János Farkas—a resistance fighter who was Wallenberg's companion during those desperate days in Budapest. János Farkas—a Hungarian who fought under the assumed name Péntek, worked alongside Raoul Wallenberg.

János Farkas was six years younger than Wallenberg. He had obtained a master's degree in electrical engineering, experienced the war in Hungary, hid his parents in Budapest, and was in a forced labour camp—and all three miraculously survived.

After the war, Farkas went to a Rothschild home for Hungarian refugees where he arrived with no money. But as with others in the story, he found support for a passage to Australia, where he finally landed in 1949 and lived an unassuming but full life. He never spoke about his wartime experiences, and would never watch a movie about the war, nor watch documentaries about the Holocaust. Nor did he tell anyone about his role in the resistance until his heroism was uncovered by the ABC's (Australian Broadcasting Commission)

Four Corners television program in the early 1980s. In almost four decades, he had never spoken of his deeds until a journalist came to ask.

Farkas passed away in 1987, but his son George was at the Wallenberg celebrations in Sydney, proudly bearing witness.

•••

George Farkas told the story of his father, a quiet, gentle, humble man who for 37 years never once spoke of the war or his experience in it. His experiences were part of his past and off-limits. His expressed his reason for emigrating to Australia, as it was for many Holocaust survivors, that it was the furthest place away from Europe that he could find.

For 37 years, neither his mother nor any other member of the family, nor anyone else for that matter, knew anything of his wartime experiences until 1982.

In the early 1980s, a worldwide movement to honour Wallenberg and to ascertain his real fate gained momentum. *Save Wallenberg Committees* sprang up in many countries.

Sydney was no exception, where a committee was established in Wallenberg's honour. There was much publicity about Wallenberg in the press.

Even with all the publicity about Wallenberg, George's father said nothing. In April 1982, one Friday night at his uncle's home where the family regularly gathered, his mother proudly exclaimed: 'We had big excitement at home this week. *Four Corners* interviewed Dad!'

Still his father said nothing. He enquired about how it was that they approached him.

Still his father said nothing.

It was left to his mother to provide the answers, information about which she knew absolutely nothing until the approach by the ABC—and gradually there unfolded a quite incredible story—a story generally untold, still in large part untold with the death of George's father in 1987.

In making the documentary on Wallenberg, *Four Corners* approached a person in Sydney, Peter Lorn, who had ostensibly been rescued by Wallenberg. That person said to them:

'Why are you speaking to me. Why don't you interview the person who actually saved my life? He is living here in Sydney.'

He then directed them to George's father. George goes on to say that even in the *Four Corners* programme, his father confined himself to describing Wallenberg's courage because of his modesty and because he took the view that it was a documentary on Wallenberg.

It was only in a lengthier radio programme with Radio 2BL in Sydney some weeks later, in an interview touching directly on himself, that the story came to light.

When János Farkas was interviewed by Radio 2BL, it was the first and only time that he told a small part of his story—and only when prodded by the interviewer to recount an incident when he was in the Hungarian Resistance, before joining Wallenberg. Farkas had ascertained that 50 people, both Jews and non-Jews, were detained at Budapest's Gestapo headquarters, now a museum known as the House of Terror. He set out with a fleet of trucks wearing a German uniform and informed the commandant that a named high-ranking General had ordered him to take the prisoners to another destination. Of course, he had no papers to verify the General's orders. When challenged on the lack of documentation, he dared the commandant to ring the General, noting that the General would be very angry at his orders being questioned. The commandant actually picked up the telephone to do so, but seeing the determination in Farkas' eyes and the warning about the impending General's anger, he put the phone down without making the call. Farkas then drove the truck convoy out with the 50 prisoners to their freedom—an extremely dangerous exercise.

George Farkas dryly noted that had the commandant made the call, George himself would most probably not be here today.

> *The fact was that my father was, in reality, Wallenberg's right-hand man for much of the six months that Wallenberg operated in Budapest and what is even of greater significance from an historical perspective, is that he was the last person in the free world to ever see and speak to Wallenberg immediately before the Soviets took him. In fact, the last words that Wallenberg ever uttered in freedom were to my father and they proved to be regrettably prophetic words indeed.*

George's father had originally been placed in a forced labour camp where he pretended to have epilepsy and, after feigning an epileptic fit, was taken to a hospital, from where he escaped.

He then joined the Hungarian Resistance and approached Wallenberg and asked to join him on his mission. He used a false name on false ID papers. George had the very photograph of him that appeared on his false ID papers in 1944. He deliberately did not reveal that he was Jewish to Wallenberg as he was afraid that Wallenberg would then refuse his approach on the grounds of it being too dangerous for a Jew to be actively involved.

> *My father went virtually everywhere with Wallenberg, accompanying him to the railway platforms and under the gaze of the German armed soldiers, thrusting Swedish papers into hands desperately reaching out of the still open doors of the wagons and hauling the recipients out and claiming immunity and protection and taking them away, in spite of threats to their own safety.*

George's dad described Wallenberg as being available day and night to assist Jews. When the 120-kilometre death marches occurred, Wallenberg set up checkpoints along the route. When a convoy of bedraggled people arrived, Wallenberg and his father would jump into his car with other aides and haul people out of the convoy. It undoubtedly took enormous nerve and courage.

George's father described Wallenberg as a handsome, very softly spoken man but a man who would argue with German officers on station platforms and who sometimes became so angry and forceful that he would either jump on a table or thump his fist on it, demanding the release of Jews into his custody. He successfully intimidated the Germans, who seemed to hold him in awe.

His real nemesis, however, was Adolf Eichmann, who had been sent to Budapest to implement the Final Solution. A personal contest developed between Wallenberg and Eichmann, who is reported to have specifically said that he wanted Wallenberg killed.

At a very genteel dinner at which both were guests, Eichmann issued an icy threat to Wallenberg. He said, 'You have a Swedish passport, but you can't be sure that it will protect you. Even a neutral diplomat can meet with an accident.' A few days later, a large German truck drove into Wallenberg's car, which was totally destroyed, but Wallenberg was not in the car.

According to George:

> *As to my father being the last person in the free world to see or speak to Wallenberg, in January 1945 the Soviets summoned Wallenberg to their headquarters. My father repeatedly tried to prevail upon him not to go, telling him that his life could be in danger as their intentions were not known.*

However, Wallenberg being the diplomat that he was, insisted on going on the basis that he was a Swedish diplomat and the Russians as the occupying forces had summoned him. As Wallenberg was about to get into the car, János Péntek, as he was known, made a last fruitless attempt to stop him.

It was then that Wallenberg uttered those, in hindsight, dreadfully foretelling words as the last words he ever uttered to anyone in the free world. He said: 'I don't know whether I'll be received as a friend or an enemy'.

And with those words, he disappeared, never to be seen outside the Soviet Union again.

> *When my father was asked, in the interview, whether he thought Wallenberg had any foreboding of what was in store for him, he said that from the look in Wallenberg's eyes when he said those fateful words, he thinks that Wallenberg had a pretty good idea of which of the two alternatives was the more likely.*

History is a witness to how he was received and treated. Notwithstanding the Soviet's contention that Wallenberg died in a Russian prison in July 1947, there were sightings of him in Soviet prisons in 1951, 1952, 1957 and 1959; in a Soviet hospital unwell in 1961; in Lubyanka prison in 1963 (the very prison where he had allegedly died in 1947); in 1975 a Swede was seen in a Soviet hospital who had been in prison for 30 years; and there are eyewitness reports to his being seen alive in Soviet prisons in the 1980s.

Doctor and patient

János Farkas refused to write a book or follow up with further media. He didn't want to be conspicuous. He didn't seek the limelight. He didn't want any attention. He didn't regard what he did as anything extraordinary, but as simply a reaction to extraordinary times that many others in his position would have also done.

János Farkas died with the major part of his story untold, forever lost to historians, biographers, libraries and museums. With him, silence consumed all the stories he had to tell. All the memories he had never shared with my uncle Nándor—who, like Farkas, had landed in Sydney and led a complete life. The two men were fast friends all throughout my childhood.

These two men, a doctor and a patient, and friends for decades in Australia, were prominent members of the Sydney Hungarian community. They spoke about all manner of things, but never their past.

Decades later, as I was writing about Wallenberg, I heard that story about how the ABC *Four Corners* journalists came knocking on the Farkas's door to talk about his wartime pursuits with Wallenberg.

As those stories were revealed, János Farkas's relationship with my uncle Nándor came to light, and the story of the Farkas family, that George now bears witness to, led me back to my own.

Chapter Eight
House of Terror and Those Shoes

House of Terror

In 2023, we visit one of the main boulevards of Budapest, the centre of fashion and European chic. There we find both the house of the composer Liszt and the magnificent Hungarian State Opera House where *Madama Butterfly* was currently playing. Then we come across a sign that spells out TERROR in large, bold open-cut letters. As we enter, we see the letters are designed to let light in through the roof of the building to lessen the gloom. As we purchase our entry tickets, we are given a brochure with the words:

'The past must be acknowledged'—*Attila József.*

Indeed, we are here to acknowledge the past, even if it is full of horror and includes some of the lowest points in Hungary's history.

Before us is the neo-Renaissance building at 60 Andrássy út which has been transformed into a museum that is now known as the House of Terror.

According to witness testimony, this building was truly 'a house of terror' when it first functioned as the headquarters of the notorious Arrow Cross who established the torture chambers in the basement.

The Nationalist Socialist movement's notorious Szálasi branch rented space in the building from 1937. The head of the Arrow Cross Party, Ferenc Szálasi, declared that 'the headquarters will always remain for me and the Hungarian popular program the *House of Loyalty.*'

The Arrow Cross mirrored their Nazi allies in their approach to interrogation and betrayal of human rights.

Their replacements weren't much better. In 1945, when Hungary was under Communist occupation, the Soviets rolled their tanks into Andrássy Boulevard. They established the Department of Political Police (PRO) when they took over the abandoned Arrow Cross Headquarters, which later became the State Security Office (ÁVO) and then the State Security Authority (ÁVH). Péter Gábor was head of all three organisations. The country learned to fear the tailor's apprentice and his terror compatriots. They were dreaded and despised; they killed without hesitation, or on the strength of extorted confessions and brutal interrogations, then sent their victims to the gallows, to prisons and labour camps.

On entering this building, you are greeted by a huge tank which dominates the confined space. That in itself would evoke fear, as it did for the Hungarians at various times in their history when confronted by both German and Russian tanks.

There are artifacts and videos on the various floors of the building that tell the story of the horrors, but it is in the basement where you can most strongly sense the torture and confinement that occurred in the various prison cells.

***

Just as a country's flag might tell a story about what is important, there is a lot that can be learned from a symbol. The insignia of a political party can tell a tale of history, of message and purpose, through an image. In fact, some images, such as the Nazi swastika, have been banned in many jurisdictions, such as where I live in the State of Victoria in Australia, as it is in Germany. The Arrow Cross is a symbol of a Hungarian Political Party that ruled with ferocity and terror from 15 October 1944 till 28 March 1945 when it was dissolved, and the reign of terror was ended. It is outlawed in modern-day Hungary.

The Arrow Cross Party (in Hungarian literally the Nyilaskeresztes Párt), NYKP, and in the Hungarian common vernacular the 'Nyilas', were dreaded 'terrorists' whose horrific assaults match those of the worst acts by latter-day terrorists, including dehumanising acts of brutality, pillage, rape and mass murder. Their symbol is the green four-pointed cross embedded in a circle, which in turn is embedded in a red shield complete with the nationalist colours of Hungary: red, white, and green. The party was founded by Ferenc Szálasi in 1939, and it was grounded in the philosophy of pro-German extremists, such as that of Gyula Gömbös, who coined the term 'national socialism'.

There are several theories about the Nyilaskeresztes. Some say just as the swastika alluded to racial purity of a people, this also alluded to that racial purity of the Magyars. It was considered to symbolise the will to nullify the Treaty of Trianon under which Hungary had lost one third of its territory after World War I, and from here on expand the Hungarian state in all directions to the borders of the former kingdom of Hungary. It combined a heap of 'isms' such as nationalism, promotion of agriculture, anti-capitalism, anti-communism and a special type of antisemitism called a-Semitism—that is, a society completely devoid of Jews.

The 1930s were tough times in Europe and elsewhere in the world and that is when the party started to dominate in working-class neighbourhoods. The Arrow Cross leadership, some being well-educated, recruited members from the poorest in society, including the long-term unemployed, alcoholics, ex-convicts, prisoners, rapists and the uneducated. A great seeding ground for the most brutal of crimes.

For the founder and subsequent leader, the ideology subscribed to the notion of the 'master race' which included Germans and Hungarians. Added to this was a concept of 'Hungarism'. A coalition of military officers and soldiers, nationalists, and agricultural workers who won 15 per cent of the vote in 1939, giving the Arrow Cross party 29 seats in the Hungarian Parliament at that time. Soon after this, Regent Horthy banned the party at the outbreak of World War II, forcing them to be clandestine. But in 1944, Hitler lost patience with Horthy and his moderate Prime Minister, Miklós Kállay, who was reluctant to fully support the Nazi line. So, in March 1944, when the German army rolled into Hungary, causing Kállay to flee the Nazi 'proxy' rule, Döme Sztójay replaced him. That led to the quick legalisation of the Arrow Cross.

During the spring and summer of 1944, more than 400,000 were driven into centralised ghettos and then deported from the Hungarian countryside to death camps. This was done by the Nazis with the 'enthusiastic' assistance of the Hungarian Interior Ministry and the gendarmerie, both of which had close links with members of the Arrow Cross. In Budapest, Jews were forced into 'Yellow Star Houses' which were a single building, somewhat like a 'mini ghetto' identified by a yellow star at the entrance. As previously noted, in August 1944, Horthy did try to stop the deportations and force the radical anti-Semites out of his government.

As the summer progressed and the Allied and Soviet armies were closing in on central Europe, the Nazis were devoting fewer resources to the 'Jewish Solution' and the Arrow Cross stepped up their efforts to fill the shortfall. They rounded up Jews in the streets and would take the children away from their parents and beat or kill any child or parent who protested. The tragic result was that there were lots of children collected in the streets of Budapest whose parents had been taken away. The Red Cross was active in picking these children up and placing them in homes.

Shoes on the Bank of the Danube

This was the time of the mass murders by the Danube River. It was a preferred execution spot of the fascists because the swift current would sweep away the body of a victim who'd toppled from the riverbank after being shot. It was considered to be an 'added bonus' that the freezing water would quickly finish off those who'd survived their gunshot wounds. Brutality and pragmatism reigned. With ammunition being in short supply, the Arrow Cross started using techniques such as tying people together with wire at the wrist and shooting only the middle person in the head. That way the unfortunate victims would drown in the Danube, dragged down by the bodies of their friends and family, while the fascists saved on bullets.

Often the Arrow Cross would force their victim, or more accurately, victims, to take off their shoes and neatly line them up on the bank before execution. After all, this was wartime, and shoes were a valuable commodity that could be traded for food or other luxuries.

Today, since 2005, a pile of shoes remains on the banks of the Danube, the site of the massacre. The shoes on the banks of the Danube are in bronze—a really unique and unassuming sculpture that stretches for metres with some 60 pairs of shoes, conceived by film director, János Can Togay, and sculptor Gyula Pauer—big and small, male and female, adult and child. There are boots and bootees, sensible solid heels, and flatties. The Hungarians always valued sensible shoes. The 60 pairs of shoes symbolise what was ordered to be left behind, possibly to be resold as the owners would no longer be there to claim them.

In fact, they are not a sculpture but a memorial of a most, if not *the* most chilling period of Hungary's history. The sculpture represents the shoes worn by many of the 3,500 people who were shot into the river Danube. Some walked to the banks of the river without shoes from as far as 60 Andrássy út, which is a long way without shoes or clothing in the particularly cold winter of December 1944.

The sculpture is not visible from the street. The shoes are out of sight, down the embankment between two entry points that lead to the river's edge. There are no signposts or markers, as if we are somewhat reluctantly allowed to confront the past. Once you do find those shoes, there is a plaque:

> *To the memory of the victims shot into the Danube by the Arrow Cross militiamen in 1944-1945.*

As others have noted, and my family registers as we stand on the bank, there is no mention that the majority of these victims were Jews. Another silence that echoes through the past. This brings home a striking realisation: Despite the pain that one carries across generations, it is your own pain that you have to deal with when confronted by harsh realities.

My own father had a lucky escape from death in the very spot I stood. In 1944, he was amongst those marched to the banks of the Danube and held at gunpoint. But, somehow, he was spared. Sadly, as a result of that near-death experience, my father always seemed aged beyond his years. He remained in ill health for the rest of his life till his passing at 53 years of age. Although he survived that moment of brutality, the rest of his life was marked by it—to what extent, not even I, as his child, will fully understand. What survival had cost him, how it came to be, he never told me. Most likely, it was my uncle who came to the rescue. Neither my father nor my uncle would ever speak of the event.

***

It was estimated that in the autumn of 1944, there were no more than 4,000 members of the Arrow Cross in Budapest terrorising a population of one million people. It is difficult to imagine that their methods became even too sickening for the German military, when General Karl Pfeffer-Wildenbruch, who was in command of the German forces during the Battle for Budapest (24 December to 11 February, 1945), ordered his men not to take part in the killings. But his authority was overridden when, as the German envoy, he received orders to supply and help the Arrow Cross as much as they could.

By October 1944, Horthy had negotiated a ceasefire with the Soviets and ordered the Hungarian troops to lay down their arms, but the Germans took Horthy into 'protective custody' in Germany and forced him to abdicate. Szálasi was made leader of the nation as Prime Minister of a Government of National Unity the same day. Meanwhile, Soviet and Romanian forces were well within the Hungarian borders.

In under three months, the death squads killed as many as 38,000 Hungarians. Eichmann restarted deportations, sending 80,000 out of Budapest into slave labour.

The Red Army reached the outskirts of Budapest in December 1944, and the siege of Budapest began. As the control of the city's institutions weakened the Arrow Cross focused on the weakest, including patients in two Jewish Hospitals on Maros Street and Bethlen Square.

The Arrow Cross maintained their attacks and many Jews were saved only through the collective efforts of a handful of Jewish leaders, foreign diplomats like Raoul Wallenberg, the Papal Nuncio Monsignor Angelo Rotta, Swiss Consul Lutz, Spanish Consul Angel Sanz Briz, and the Italian cattle trader Georgio Perlasca. As well as the heretofore lesser-known persons that I had become interested in, Nándor Eichel and János Farkas.

The Arrow Cross government fell at the end of January 1945 when the Soviet army took Pest and the German forces retreated across the Danube to Buda.

Szálasi had escaped Budapest on 11 December 1944, taking with him the Hungarian royal crown, the Holy Crown, also known as the Crown of Saint Stephen, named in honour of Saint Stephen I of Hungary. This was the coronation crown used by the Kingdom of Hungary for most of its existence; kings had been crowned with it since the 12th century.

The Crown is considered to be one of the most important symbols in Hungarian history. It symbolised the King's authority, along with the pride and nationalism expressed in the concept of Hungarianness. Throughout the history of Hungary, more than 50 kings were crowned with it, until 1916 and the last king, Charles IV. In 1945, the crown was taken to the United States and returned from the USA on 6 January 1978, by Secretary of State Cyrus Vance. It is now sitting in the magnificent parliament building, proudly displayed to the throngs of admiring visitors.

Back in the Szálasi period, the history of beautiful Budapest reads like a horror story. In Budapest, it is the House of Terror where the atrocities of the Arrow Cross are recorded. But below, some other stories are recorded.

Please turn away or close your eyes if you do not want to read about what might seem both improbable and impossible.

Or, please consider a mental health warning, also known as a trigger warning, for those who read these pages.

A footnote here. Sadly in 2025 these stories are not in the past. There have been atrocities by ISIS and Hamas to remind us of what humans can and still do to others.

Having read these stories carefully you might want to then turn to the internet for verification. The facts are there. The stories are not new, and indeed, there could be some 3,500 to 8,000 or 10,000 of these stories. The exact numbers were never recorded. Two of the stories come from people whom I know well, and for me, they do not need verification as they are in the public domain; the third is from an academic whose book is readily available and who has been motivated to explore the happenings of that era for personal reasons.

Arrow Cross Stories
Peter's Story

My friend Peter Halas records his mother's story. In 1942 his father was conscripted to a labour camp to work digging trenches and doing other support work for the army. His father survived the winters in minus 20–30 degrees Celsius because his job was to drive a truck, and it was the cabin of the truck that kept him warm. His brothers did not survive.

Peter's grandparents feared that worse was to come, so they went into hiding. Five-year-old Peter and his mother were hidden by Armenian friends who took a great risk, as they would have suffered the same fate as the Jews if they were caught. They lived on potatoes and beans. It was his maternal grandfather's birthday on 15 December, so his mother took off her yellow star (front and back) and insisted on visiting her father, defying the curfew which forbade Jews to be in the streets after 4 pm. That was the last time that Peter saw his mother.

The grandparents' building was raided by the Arrow Cross. They collected all the Jews and marched them to the river Danube and shot them all.

News about what had happened on the banks of the Danube came via a young boy, who was amongst those taken to the river. He begged the Nazi not to shoot him as he was just a young kid. The young Arrow Cross operative had kicked him in the butt, and he fell into the river before the shooting started. He waited till it was all over, clambered out and came back to tell those who needed to know what had happened.

Peter's own survival story had a good ending. The couple who were looking after him feared for their own lives, so they went with him to look for alternate shelter. After walking what seemed like hours, they arrived on the outskirts of Budapest where they were met by a couple they knew who had no children and were willing to hide him.

By that time the Soviet Army was closing in on the German Army. The Americans were bombing Budapest from the air, and the Soviets were advancing on the ground. As the bombings were constant, they ran to the cellar each time the air raid siren went off, not knowing if the building above them would be hit. Food was hard to get. He remembers the excitement when a horse was shot and the whole neighbourhood rushed onto the street and butchered it. The man he was staying with went out one night and walked to the Soviet lines where he begged them for food. He remembers him coming back with sausages, which were considered to be a feast.

Early in 1945, the Battle of Budapest was won by the Allies, but it was not till June of that year that his father returned to the family.

Suzanne's story

Suzanne Nozick, in her interview and testimony to the Spielberg Archives, describes a happy childhood where she was brought up in 'cotton wool', protected from hardships, that is, until she was 18 years old. The family lived in a beautiful apartment that today would be called a penthouse. She had spent time at a finishing school in Switzerland and went to France to learn French. Her uncle went to university in the 1930s and already experienced antisemitism when he was attacked for being Jewish. By then, Jews already had difficulty getting jobs. Her architect father was taken to one of those forced labour camps, as the Jews were not allowed to bear arms, so their labour was used for digging trenches and in other support work for the army. He was never seen again.

Things changed on 19 March 1944. It was a Sunday morning in spring when a friend who was staying with Suzanne was called home because the Germans had arrived. First, they took their bicycles away; then they had to hand in their jewellery, and then they were ordered to leave their flat with only what they had in their hands. Suzanne describes how she was holding a broom at the time, so she marched down Árpád Street with a broom!! She says, 'Just shows how little we knew about what was happening'. They first moved into the three-bedroom house which belonged to her uncle. Many families were there. It was a protected house, with a yellow star.

Later she joined her mother in a large six- or seven-story apartment building. There was a lot of bombing by the British, so they spent much of the time in the cellar. During the nights the Arrow Cross regularly came with threats to shoot, calling them terrible names and intimidating them. One time, they forced her grandfather to carry books from the first floor to the sixth floor in what seemed a fruitless task that exhausted him.

Suzanne's family knew they had to leave, so she arranged for her and her mother, Ibolya, to hide in a hospital where she had worked briefly as a laboratory assistant after finishing school, and knew the professor who was a director. The hospital, too, proved not to be safe.

Suzanne recalls that on 13 February, when the Soviet and Romanian forces had encircled Budapest and were close to liberating the city, 'Four soldiers in black uniforms carrying guns stormed in where 14 of them were hiding in one room'. She showed them her false papers, but that did not work, so they belted her around the head till she saw stars. They were marched to 60 Andrássy Boulevard—the Gestapo/Arrow Cross House (now the aforementioned House of Terror).

They were taken from the hospital to the cellar at 60 Andrássy út where they were held for three days. Professor Lénárd, who had been her teacher at the hospital in happier times, had his eyes beaten out in the cellar with a screwdriver in front of them. Suzanne witnessed a lot of people dying in that cellar. There were interrogations, beatings, rapes, starvation, and tortures of the most horrible kind. They accused her of being a 'communist whore' and a 'stinking Jew'. They beat her till she nearly lost consciousness.

Being a young, good-looking female, Suzanne was kicked to the middle of the cellar where a piece of wood was inserted into her. They beat her and her mother with whips. When the two women fainted, they poured water onto them, and when they regained consciousness, they beat them again. Mother and daughter hugged each other, which provoked their tormentors to start again. They put paper between Suzanne's legs and toes and lit it. Ibolya's head was forced into a toilet with excrement, which she had to swallow.

> *They raped me and my mother too. They raped all the women. When I fainted, they thew water over me. They kept beating us with whips when we regained consciousness. They put a rubber thing in me between my legs.*
>
> *Then they brought some more people into the cellars. They were Gypsies. They were given the same treatment as us. They were beaten and raped too. The Gypsies had to 'make sex' with us on the floor while the Arrow Cross boys watched. They killed him [while he was] on me and they laughed.*

After three days of torture, they were marched naked to the banks of the Danube, which was a long way, especially in minus 15 degrees. The Arrow Cross operatives were behind them with guns. Suzanne was holding her mother's hand. They were not allowed to talk. She asked, 'Why were we not allowed to talk if they knew they were going to kills us?' The man behind her asked her, 'Nice Rebecca, (because it is a Jewish name) can you swim?' Ibolya seemed resigned to an end to her ordeal, and thought, 'Your father must be dead, your mother must be dead—it is not the worst thing that is going to happen to us'. Her story follows in her own words.

> *As a 19-year-old I knew we were going to be shot. I still hoped. We arrived there and we were shot. I must have fallen into the Danube, or the Arrow Cross didn't shoot. It was pitch dark, very quiet. I got myself out after a while. It was all ice. Then I walked. I heard some German soldiers coming to me. 'Let her rot; let her freeze to death. That's more painful than to put a bullet in her.' I was unconscious for a while then some Hungarian soldiers found me. I couldn't walk. There were two or three of them. They took me to the Hungarian soldiers' barracks. Being naked they put a blanket on me. I was shivering and crying. They gave me brandy, and I slept. The next day they said, 'The Russians are very close, you can hear them. We can't stay here in the barracks.' They had to run away from the Russians, and I can't go with them because I can't walk. I pleaded 'Don't give me back to the Arrow Cross rather shoot me here. My mother was shot, it doesn't matter anymore.' They said they were going to take me to the ghetto. I was quite happy to go to the ghetto hospital and one of the Jewish doctors Groszman — ... he was a children's specialist who had taken my tonsils out and he gave me two lumps of sugar and then the Russians came on 21 January. Liberation. And my grandmother found me. She asked, 'Where is Ibolya [her mother]?' And I had to tell her she was shot. My grandfather died from typhus in the hospital. There was no food at that time in Hungary. There were no shops. We were so hungry.*

The man who would later become her husband located a sleigh, as she still couldn't walk and took her to friends in Újpest. There had been a lot of looting of the family apartments, supposedly by the Russian soldiers. The family apartment had been cleared of everything, including the parquetry floors being chopped up for firewood. Suzanne continued into all the family apartments. *'I went into every flat I took out things. I didn't really want them; but I remember they belonged to my father.'*

As for my family's story, there was no oral or written testimony to refer to, just a code of silence, unspoken and unrecorded in the public domain. It was only when I started researching my family's history that I learned a little of what happened during those months of terror under the Arrow Cross.

In August 1944, Horthy appointed the anti-fascist general Géza Lakatos, to be prime minister, and the Hungarian military was ordered to prevent any further Hungarian citizens from being deported. The reprieve for the Jewish population was short-lived. The Horthy regime fell on 15 October 1944 and was replaced by the Nazi-backed Arrow Cross Party headed by Ferenc Szálasi. During the next few months, over 70,000 Jews were shot or deported to death camps.

On 29 November 1944, the Budapest ghetto was established. It was surrounded by a high fence and stone wall and was heavily guarded. Even Jews who had protection certificates were moved into the ghetto, which contained 162 apartment houses and two synagogues. Like other ghettos established in Europe, it was completely cut off from the outside world, with no food allowed in and no rubbish transported out; dead bodies were left to pile up outside the bombed-out store fronts.

During periods of particularly high risk, Nándor and his family were able to take shelter at the Swiss Embassy. The story is told that one day, an Arrow Cross operative entered the Embassy and threatened to shoot everyone. Nándor covered Robert for protection. They were saved when a member of the foreign office, perhaps Mr Weiss or Lutz himself, made it clear to the operative that the Embassy was protected Swiss territory and not part of Hungary. That may well have been the raid that was described by Andor Schwarz. Following this narrow escape, Nándor and the family remained in the Swiss consulate for the remaining weeks of the war.

The Arrow Cross continued to hunt down Jewish people hiding and living on false papers. Between December 1944 and the end of January 1945, the Arrow Cross took as many as 20,000 Jews from the ghetto and shot them on the shores of the Danube or in the streets of Budapest.

Towards the end of 1944, when the Hungarian government realised it was going to lose the war, Nándor was asked to move 70 Jewish people to safety. They were to move to a protected house on a particular Sunday morning, but, at 9 am that day, acting on an instinct, Nándor decided to delay their departure. Half an hour later, the 'safe' house was bombed, and all the inhabitants were killed.

Three months after the ghetto was established, on 13 February 1945, the Soviet army liberated Hungary after a 50-day siege known as the Battle of Budapest. From occupation to liberation, the Jewish population of Hungary was reduced from approximately 825,000 to only 260,000, with half surviving in the countryside and half in Budapest[1] many of whom survived due to humanitarians like Carl Lutz and Swedish envoy Raoul Wallenberg. It is becoming clearer now that Nándor's judgement and good fortune also saved the lives of many Jews.

Between 1945 and 1946, the city had to be rebuilt. A handful of images survive from that time: the streets were rubble, the soldier on a bicycle, with a gun hoisted over his shoulder and wearing a hard hat. Was he a Russian? Burnt bodies being collected, smoke billowing from burning buildings. Two elderly hatted men watch on in disbelief; the Russian soldiers in their long winter coats with bayonets at the ready, shovel on back also at the ready, storm through the rubble in a group, bringing terror to the population, just in case someone wanted to challenge their presence. The Hungarian soldiers with their guns at the ready were not a match for the Russians. Other soldiers stand sentinel against the war-ravaged buildings of the beautiful city. And the Lánchid or Chain Bridge, as it is known to tourists, stands collapsed in the Danube as the frozen river keeps watch. Spring comes, and the river that was filled with blood flows clear and smoothly again.

Who will forget the rivers of blood? The pictures tell the tale.

***

As I was writing this book the stories kept flooding in. People I have known all my life, but only had scant knowledge of their personal histories. Books that had been published, a webinar that told a personal history, testimonies in museums and the Spielberg archives and memoirs that had been written. I knew precious little about my own family's experiences, but there are countless horrors to write about, more than those of my friends and their parents. I have chosen just a few.

In a webinar, László Borhi (Webinar 12 December 2021) historian from Indiana University, recounts how on Christmas Day, 1944, around midnight, a detachment of armed Arrow Cross servicemen located a few blocks from Arrow Cross headquarters, went to the Silesian Institute where they suspected monks were hiding Jewish children. He describes them as carrying out biological screening of the six- to 15-year-old males, presumably to see whether they were circumcised, and they were able to pick up two boys.

Only one boy survived when taken to the Danube. Before the shot was fired, the boy asked if there was any mercy and when he was told no, he just jumped into the river, and that was László Borhi's father. On the hills of Buda, they also raided the Convent of the Sisters of the Divine Love where the targets were little girls. They also went through biological screening, looking at their profiles, anything that would identify them as Jews or having a disability, which is a eugenics approach to things. Only two had had mental illness. Borhi describes the atrocities as having been created in 'Hungary's workshop'. A relatively few thousand terrorised a city of a million people.

The number of casualties will never be known, but the estimates of 3,500 to 8,000 don't include the physically and psychologically maimed.

Many in the Arrow Cross went back to normal life if they escaped the postwar trials of the 1940s and the two Arrow Cross trials of the 1960s. Borhi describes the Arrow Cross as having an ideology of hatred. None were born killers; they didn't kill before the war or after the war. Some had antisemitic animus. Some bragged about the number that they took to the river. They had regrets that they did not kill more. There is a narrative that Hungary was Hitler's last ally. Borhi explains how it is all fuelled by antisemitism and envy of the other, which he describes as a 'murderous Judeophobia and class resentment.' In the eyes of their persecutors, Jews were more like dogs who could creep and crawl.

The Arrow Cross and German forces continued to fight a rear-guard action in the far west of Hungary till April 1945. People's courts were established under the leadership of long-time military judge, Colonel Ákos Major. Postwar there were no less than 6,200 indictments for murder served against the Arrow Cross in just a few months. There were many executions, including Szálasi. By the time they were disbanded in 1950, approximately 26,000 people were convicted for treason, war crimes, or crimes against humanity during their reign of terror.

Atrocities happened under Hungary's gaze. The trials of the Arrow Cross leadership and operatives continued in the second half of the 1940s and some in the 1960s.

The verdict in 1948 according to one judge cited by Borhi, said. 'The perpetrators were the Hungarian executioners and servants of raging Hitlerism. During the siege of Budapest, the police were intimidated by Arrow Cross militia. The Party leaders did not ask for atrocities but didn't stop it.'

So, a harsh judgement has been made on not only the perpetrators, but upon those who failed to stop the atrocities.

Part 3

'Hope is the memory of the future.'

—Elie Wiesel

Chapter 9
In Australia

The Sydney Chevra Kadisha

A funeral is generally a sombre event. In a Jewish gathering, there are no flowers, no music; just prayers and a eulogy to celebrate the life of the deceased. In Jewish tradition, it's considered healing for those who are left behind to share tales that may not have been known by the mourners in attendance.

Consider the funeral of János Farkas, born in May 1918, who passed away at the relatively young age of 67. Before the body is laid to rest at the bleak, distant Rookwood Cemetery, there is at first a service at the Sydney Chevra Kadisha, the Jewish funeral parlour. The words 'Chevra Kadisha' literally translate to Sacred Society, but since the 19th century, the name refers to a burial society made up of men and women who look after the body of the deceased, washing and cleaning it until it is ready for the full service at the local Chevra Kadisha.

As you drive through Bondi Junction along the edge of Centennial Park—past where gentle horse-riding still takes place,, there is an interesting building: the Sydney Chevra Kadisha. It is made in that dark red brick so familiar to Sydneysiders. The foundation stone was laid in 1948 by Rabbi Porush who was the senior Rabbi at the Great Synagogue in Sydney. It is a rather long building set at an angle with a pointy end. Inside, the walls are white, minus any decorative features; just one small circular stained-glass window where the speaker stands, surrounded by the heavy mahogany timber which provides a welcome piece of colour for the eye. The heavy timber pews are where the mourners and their relatives and friends sit. The clear windows are accentuated by a stained-glass window above each panel.

I was only in there on one occasion, and that was in 1962 at the passing of my own father. It was where the prayers and eulogies were said. I was 18 at the time and dealing with the grief and the loss, sitting in the front row alongside my mother and teenage sister, so was not aware of the number of people behind me.

It was the same building where George Farkas would have heard the Rabbi deliver his father's significant eulogy describing the exploits of János Farkas, the quiet, unassuming man going under the name of Péntek. János Farkas, who was Wallenberg's right-hand man, a partisan who had escaped and helped others to escape wearing an Arrow Cross uniform.

The family sit in the front rows as the mourners pile in, taking their seats. Some early comers choose to express their condolences to the grieving family before being seated. The coffin, always closed, is in full view, draped with a black cloth, untouched or visited by the mourners who sit waiting for the proceedings to begin. The silence is generally palpable.

At the funeral of János Farkas, the Rabbi, begins his eulogy, much of the detail in the script most likely provided by George, describing the father as ' ... a quiet, extremely modest, and very humble man who for 37 years, like many other survivors, never spoke of the war or of his experiences of it, that is, until 1982, and then only briefly.'

The Rabbi told the story of János Farkas's wartime service in a forced labour camp, as was the fate of the men of that time. He feigned an epileptic fit, was taken to a hospital from where he escaped and joined the partisan activities. He took on an assumed name, Péntek, a common Hungarian name meaning 'Friday', with false identification documents so that he could join Wallenberg's rescue mission. Not declaring his Jewishness made him less of a target when working with Wallenberg. Perhaps Friday was the day he had made that decision to join? Perhaps it was an homage to Daniel Defoe's character 'my man Friday' in the 1719 novel, *Robinson Crusoe*, taking on a new identity to survive impossible circumstances.

In the early 1980s there was a great deal of media interest in Raoul Wallenberg and his rescue activities in wartime Budapest. It was in 1982 when the aforementioned *Four Corners* television crew from the local broadcaster wanted to record the Wallenberg story. They had links with Wallenberg's driver. That man told the television crew to interview the man who was always with Wallenberg, and that was a man called János Farkas.

The Rabbi recounted the 2BL radio interview where the story of the rescue of the 50 captives from Budapest headquarters came to light.

Péntek, the man now known as Farkas, went virtually everywhere with Wallenberg, under the gaze of the Nazi occupiers. He has been described as Wallenberg's right-hand man for much of the six months that Wallenberg operated in Budapest. It would have meant a great deal of activity in open view of all.

He spoke of the fate of Wallenberg, and the fact that Péntek was the last person in the free world to speak to Wallenberg before the Soviets took him.

The Rabbi talked about the Farkas parents' meeting and subsequent marriage in Paris in 1948, their travels to Australia and how they lived a quiet and prosperous life in Sydney's beautiful Rose Bay.

He described János as the quiet, unassuming man who had refused to write a book or engage with the media. He had considered that what he had done was simply what others would have done, and had done, under extraordinary circumstances.

He died, with a major part of his life story not recorded in libraries or museums.

At the end of the service, the family doctor Nándor Eichel goes up to George and says:

> *Now you see how humble your father was. I was his doctor and friend for 30 years and he confided just about everything to me. In all that time, he never mentioned one word of his wartime deeds, which I heard for the first time today.*

Both men could be described as humble and silent about their wartime activities. There was never any denial, but neither was there ever any conversation about it, despite the comfortable doctor–patient relationship. Indeed, as the Farkas family continued to be the patients of Nándor Eichel, the good doctor never discussed or disclosed his wartime activities to George on any subsequent occasion.

Nándor also chose not to relive and share his experiences as a record for perpetuity in the Spielberg archival records. It was only as, one by one, individuals came into contact with his family did they acknowledge that Nándor had saved their lives.

Getting out

Nándor, on his wedding day, was not particularly tall, just lean, and he matched his bride in height; or was she standing on a step to look taller? Photographers used such tricks in those days (and perhaps even today). The wedding invitation was a simple but printed one announcing that on 24 November 1940, there would be a wedding at the Orthodox Kazinczy Street Synagogue. The telegrams were to be addressed to the bride's family Bernáth at Dohány utca 56. The very street where the most famous of Budapest's Synagogues stands.

As a young father, Nándor was slim, with a goatee beard that he retained from his wedding day in November 1940 till he left Nefelejcs Street behind. He had a quick gait, like someone who had lots to do and in a hurry to do it. He was self-assured and offered a half smile on his resting face. The other half of his appearance was one of a man with a purpose who knew what he was doing, thus inspiring confidence and trust in others. As a child and later as an adult, Nándor always appeared to me to be a man who was on the move. His mind was ticking over; he was energetic and exuded wisdom as he offered a succinct piece of advice. He was not a socialiser or a man of excessive words.

As the years rolled on for both of us, his demeanour took on a warm, paternal appearance with an air of authority. He was always smartly dressed, in the heat of Sydney summer in a short-sleeved shirt, but generally in a suit. He was clean-shaven, and no one would have guessed that in his youth he had studied to be a rabbi. He always remained a truly Orthodox man without sporting a beard or wearing external tell-tale garb. Not once do I recall seeing him wear casual clothes. There was no collection of shoes; sneakers were not yet in fashion. It was formal attire for informal occasions.

...

Nándor had made plans for his family, which now included a baby girl named Judy (Yudka), to leave Hungary but on 11 December 1948, he received an order from the Russian authorities to assemble with his family at a certain location in Budapest. Nándor's headstrong and cautious wife, Pesza, suggested not showing up as ordered. Instead, the family packed and secretively left the country that day, leaving behind their three-bedroom home and most of their belongings. The family boarded a train at the Budapest terminal, and they set off for Paris. The mistrust of the authorities was most likely warranted.

Nándor later spoke of his mother, my grandmother, accompanying them to the train, knowing that her son, daughter-in-law and grandchildren would most likely be lost to her forever. She would later endure another emotional farewell when she said goodbye to my mother and our family in Paris. After leaving Hungary, neither Nándor nor my mother saw their parents again. The distance and expense made a trip to Israel, where their parents emigrated, unlikely during those postwar years when there were careers and livelihoods to be established.

During their journey, the Eichel family were stopped at the Austrian border by the Hungarian Communists, and as the young Robert remembers, they were given a hard time but managed to get on the train. A sympathetic soldier somehow covered for them on the train and later declared that he, too, had a Jewish mother who had cried when he had left Budapest.

From Austria, Pesza, Robert and Judy went on to Paris to await their flight to Australia while Nándor went to Zurich to complete his medical degree. The plan was that he would join his family after graduating. Judy recalls that the journey to Australia included stopovers in San Francisco and Hawaii, where the family were presented with *leis*, the traditional flowery necklace Hawaiians greet visitors with. Perhaps they were travelling as VIPs.

Upset that his father had seemingly disappeared, and typically mischievous, seven-year-old Robert announced that he hoped the plane would crash.

Upon their arrival in Sydney, the family was greeted by a representative from a Jewish Welfare Group which may have been supported financially by the JDC, the American organisation that had most likely employed Nándor in Budapest, or at least supported the family. It is difficult to establish how funds are distributed in wartime and from what source, but it is clear that the JDC supported the first few years of Nándor's studies postwar in Switzerland, and also helped his family to transit to Australia, as they had done for mine, (and also, for that matter, countless others).

Pesza, Judy and Robert moved into an apartment in 12 Penkivil Lane in Bellevue Hill, near Pesza's parents, Paula, and Shmuel Bernáth. The Bernáth family, included Pesza's sisters Henda and Fritzi, brothers Joseph and Donni, and many nephews and nieces, who had settled in Sydney the previous year. The family had been sponsored by Abraham Rabinovitch, the founder of Moriah College in Sydney.

Nándor's brother, Misi and his wife Anna and their children *Ági* and *Öcs*i left Budapest eight months after Nándor's family, in August 1949. They travelled to Vienna and then to Paris where they remained for three months before leaving for Israel in November 1949.

My maternal grandparents, Eli and Giza, followed Misi's family to Israel the following year. Upon arrival, my grandparents lived in an immigration centre in Jerusalem, but after my grandfather died in 1951, my grandmother moved in with Misi's family. She later suffered from dementia and died in 1959.

In Sydney

Taking life in his stride, Nándor had studied to be a Rabbi as that was the opportunity afforded to him. He was clearly highly capable; that sort of biblical learning endeavour could challenge one at whatever level they were willing to be challenged.

Also, it is likely that he was already thinking of a people-centred career. But when it was possible, straight after the proverbial war's dust had settled, in late 1945, Nándor commenced his medical studies in Budapest.

In late 1948, when it became clear that opportunities to leave the country might close off imminently under the increasing yoke of the Communist regime, he continued studying in Switzerland, where he completed his medical studies, but not without major obstacles. At the three-year mark he was warned that in Australia, where he was heading to join his family, his Swiss credentials would not be accepted as a full medical qualification. So his internationally funded scholarship was not extended. The Australian Medical Board of the time would require him to re-sit a rigorous series of examinations over a three-year period. He was determined, and as was his way, he found support from the Swiss Government to complete his studies, which culminated in the ground-breaking research that was reported in the journal *Anaesthesia and Intensive Care* by his granddaughter in July 2017.

Nándor completed his studies in Switzerland and arrived in Sydney in 1951, one year after us. My family had joined my aunt Pesza several weeks after our arrival in Sydney in December 1950. At that time, our family of five shared one of the two bedrooms in the apartment and my aunt shared the other bedroom with her two children. The modest loungeroom was where she earned her living sewing garments. When Nándor rejoined his family, it was time for us to move out of the apartment and into our own rented family lodgings at Bondi Beach.

Nándor was required to complete his qualifications in Australia, so once again, he needed financial support which he sought from a Jewish Welfare agency. He was turned down. There would have been many immigrants in need at the time, so agencies would have been inundated with requests, and an application from a 43-year-old Rabbi, who already had a Swiss medical degree, would not have seemed a high priority. Initially, while studying in Sydney, he worked in a chocolate factory, and further support for the family most likely came from extended family and/or other benefactors. Nándor must have shown steely determination and academic promise, as in the fifth year of the Sydney medical course, the Dean of the medical school offered to find him funds to finish his studies.

Thus in 1955, he successfully completed his three-year 'bridging' course to graduate as an MD in Australia. His vocabulary did not seem to include the words, 'not possible'. He always solved problems and found solutions. Those years in Budapest would have been a good preparatory grounding for overcoming obstacles to achieve what might seem to others as quite impossible. That was followed by a one-year residency in Parramatta which was followed by work in private practice in Bankstown for two years. Those suburbs seemed very far from Bondi Beach and Bellevue Hill where the family lived.

However, in 1954, the stress in the family became evident. Like many traumatised immigrants in a family system, someone bears the scars. Or as the famous trauma psychiatrist Gábor Máté says, using the words from the title of a book by a fellow psychiatrist, Bessel van der Kolk, 'the body keeps the score'.

Máté, a Canadian, had himself as an infant been sheltered at the Glass House with his mother until it became untenable to have an infant there, forcing his 25-year-old mother to give up her baby to an unknown Christian woman for safekeeping. Both he and his mother survived the war, but on camera he admits that more than seven decades later, he continues to bear the scars of the trauma.

The psychiatric hospitals in Sydney were supporting fractured postwar victims. Many of them were women who spent extended periods in and out of hospitals, sometimes receiving the radical (and now rarely used) electroconvulsive therapy treatment (ECT, known informally as 'shock treatment').

Talking therapies were not the norm in those days, but through my own contemporary lens of an education in psychology, and the benefit of hindsight, I know that many of the parents of my friends and relatives were struggling with what we would today label as post-traumatic stress disorder (PTSD). For some, the past weighed heavily on their new lives. For others, it was the more recent stresses of life and marriage, and circumstances were sometimes too challenging.

Robert remembers his bar mitzvah at the age of 13 in 1955. His father had moved out for a year. It was a small affair in a synagogue in Roscoe Street, Bondi, close to our home in Curlewis Street. He remembers one cake, and no grandparents being present. It was still a time of considerable hardship, financial and emotional, and the stresses in the family were in full view. A stark contrast to the lavish celebrations we enjoyed in the 1980s and beyond. Robert remembers experiencing hunger and people dropping in with food. It was likely to be a time when his mother experienced a vulnerable period and spent time in hospital.

Then followed the immigrant success story. In 1957–1958, Ferdinánd Nándor Eichel fixed the shiny brass plate outside his private medical practice in Bondi Junction. First with three offices in Newland Street and again in the 1960s when he purchased a semi-detached house at 4 Ebley Street.

His business card is much as you would see today.

Dr F.N. Eichel
60 MACKENZIE STREET
BONDI JUNCTION 2022

Fred, as he was known by those who wanted to Anglicise his name, stayed in that surgery complex for 36 years, where he consulted, supported by a secretary, until 1997.

He had a thriving one-man practice with a very loyal, mainly Hungarian clientele. He was the doctor to entire families, such as the Farkases, who remember their childhood, adolescence and early adult years in his waiting room which was always filled with subdued Hungarian chatter.

He continued to live modestly in the two-bedroom flat in Penkivil Lane, Bondi, with Robert sleeping in one bedroom, and his daughter Judy on the couch in the loungeroom; not an unusual way to accommodate a family in those times.

The medical practice must have done well; debts were repaid so the savings could begin. When Robert finished his final year of high school, the family bought a black and white TV set, well after the 1956 Olympic Games. When the young Robert was in his 20s, the family moved from the Penkivil Lane rental apartment to Roslyn Street.

It was a small family home at 15 Roslyn Street, Bellevue Hill, with sufficient rooms for each child to sleep in and a garage fronting the home to house the car that was essential for a medical practitioner. Home calls or visits were the norm, and Nándor did many of those. My father, who was in poor health from the early 1950s, was visited regularly by Nándor, generally several times a week. Bondi Junction to Bondi Beach was a quick run in the car.

The house was a modest house by Bellevue Hill standards. It had no fancy distinguishing features except that one was greeted by the solid sandstone fence in natural hues, several feet high, a typical feature of the neighbourhood.

By the 1970s, when I returned from living abroad and visited, there were iron grates on the windows, much as they are today. Security had become an issue.

The Bondi building housing Nándor's practice grew old, as the doctor and his loyal clientele grew old with him. Nándor passed away on 12 April, 1998. His granddaughter, Tamara, an anaesthetist, as noted earlier, described an encounter with a patient:

When a woman came in with two secondary swollen glands which should have been treated much sooner, she asked, 'Why did you not attend to this sooner?' she said, 'there was no other doctor like him (Nándor Eichel)'. She had neglected to see another doctor after Nandor's passing.

Whenever I visited Nándor in his home, whether it was in the two-bedroom apartment in Penkivil Lane or later in Roslyn Street, what is a standout memory for me is the glass cabinet filled with gifts from appreciative patients. It was always something I admired and perhaps with a little envy, because I grew up in a household that had no art, silver, or home decorator items. It was always just basic commodities and survival, without luxuries. The gifts were displayed modestly in the glass cabinet, and he never talked about the contents unless asked. Those silver exhibits just sat sentinel in the cabinet as reminders of the gratitude of his patients.

At the cemetery, Nándor's grave has lots of pebbles on the tombstone; people have visited and placed a shiny white pebble on the tomb to mark their visit and respect, as is the Jewish custom. Also, it is a mark of the frequency that his graveside is visited.

Meeting George Farkas

My favourite part of Sydney is not the much-celebrated Bondi Beach, where I learned to surf (or more accurately, self-taught to swim after my sister dumped me in the North Bondi Baths!), but Double Bay.

It is where Hungarian is in the 'air'. It can be heard everywhere, and if not the words, then certainly the accents. At the Twenty-One Espresso Restaurant, the menu is almost entirely Hungarian; that is, the familiar Magyar cuisine.

Nándor lived not far from Double Bay in Roslyn Street, Bellevue Hill, in the early 1960s when his children were almost into adulthood; easy driving distance to his surgical practice in Bondi Junction where the atmosphere was somewhat different. Oxford Street was just one main shopping strip where the buses from Sydney Girls' High School and Randwick Boys' High School converged so that we school students, like my friends and I, could mix and mingle at the bus stop. Now the vast Westfield shopping complex dominates the landscape.

Behind this main shopping strip was Ebley Street, which intersected with Mackenzie Street, where at number 60 a modest, semi-detached building housed Nándor's surgery. There were a number of rooms where a loyal receptionist greeted people and from where the good doctor invited them into his surgery for consultation. I visited that surgery on numerous occasions; I had no need for other doctors.

This is where Nándor would meet George Farkas and his family. The patient and the doctor lived only one suburb away from one another. Bellevue Hill and Rose Bay are adjacent to one another in the beautiful Eastern Suburbs of Sydney, not too far from harbour views, if they ever had time to appreciate such niceties in their busy immigrant lives, juggling work and family.

I am not sure how I got to know George Farkas, but in the course of my research on Nándor, someone must have suggested that I contact him. It was likely to be a friend of mine who had heard of George's amazing family history in Budapest. And additionally, George and his family had been longstanding, loyal patients of Nándor Eichel in his general practice.

George's mother's family had a different story from that of his father. As war raged in Europe, her family fled Germany to Belgium where they were unsuccessful in their attempts to leave Europe, so the family went to Paris to flee the approaching Germans. The family continued to move progressively south from Paris, hiding in farmhouses, and when they suspected that the Germans were coming, they ran. His uncle was in a Gestapo prison on his 21st birthday. After the war the family went back to Paris and George's mother met his father, János, at the George V Hotel, at a Jewish function (now Four Seasons George V, one of the finest hotels in the world) Serendipitously, George was born in King George V Memorial Hospital for Mothers and Babies in Camperdown in Sydney, part of the Royal Prince Alfred Hospital complex.

Since Nándor made regular home visits, as was the common practice by family doctors in those days, he visited the Farkas home where George lived with his parents. Like Nándor, George's parents didn't have a large social life.

Were they trying to lie low, or were they just experiencing difficult times? There was family, and perhaps like my family, there were a few close friends who were considered as 'family' and with whom free moments were shared. But there were no parties or grand celebrations.

The Farkas family did frequent the Twenty-One Espresso owned by Jancsi Schiffer, a friend of George's father János from the Labour Camps in the home country.

George describes his father as a 'mild, retiring, timid guy who just did what he did because they were extraordinary times'. But there is much more to the story!!

János Farkas was involved in releasing 50 prisoners from Gestapo Headquarters. That does not seem to be the work of a shy, timid man!

Late in 2022 when I visited George, I was introduced to his house, a place with its own Jewish history. It was the location of the Young Men's Hebrew Association, known as 'the Y' in the 1940s and beyond—a property bequeathed by the Michaelis family to be used as a place to stay for refugees, that served as the Jewish Community Centre of Sydney, a reception centre for weddings, bar mitzvahs, community and cultural events.

It is so appropriate, or again serendipitous, that George is currently engaged in the rebuild of the Hakoah Club and Sports Facility at White City, a similar multipurpose sports, community and cultural hub for the Jewish Community of Sydney, expected to complete construction in 2026.

•••

I visited George Farkas hoping to learn more than what the newspaper clippings could tell me about his father.

Clearly George is a collector of antiquities; old typewriters sit near a fireman's outfit in his study, with a clear space made on his desk for work. The study and the living room walls are lined with mainly leatherbound legal volumes. The bathroom has apothecary items and the spare room holds countless items, including timber panelling from George's Chambers (office for legal practice), just in case he wants to reuse them.

A more momentous visit is described by George during our conversation. He tells the story of the photographer who came to George's house to interview five survivors. George had purchased the home in 1991, and three of the people had been in the house when it was the Y Centre, either to attend a Sunday School, play cards, tennis or attend communal functions.

As George was relating the story of his house and his family's journey from Budapest to the gathering, one photographer said he had been in Budapest at the same time as George's father.

The man had worked with Wallenberg as his bicycle courier. The man said that Wallenberg always had another man with him.

It was 60 years post the war at that time, but nevertheless George asked if the man knew his father. At first, he said 'no' until he was shown a photo taken in 1945, and he instantly recognised him. 'That's the man Wallenberg always had with him.'

The man was indeed George's father, János, who went under the aforementioned assumed name of Péntek, and who had been an 'underground' freedom fighter. George's parents came to Australia in 1949 when his mother was pregnant with him, and two years before Nándor landed.

George reminisces with me as he describes Nándor's surgery at 60 Mackenzie Street, Bondi Junction. The waiting room was always full. Everyone spoke Hungarian; there was a commonality. He remembers a 'grungy' sink in the corner which needed dusting. Empty jars were sitting on the sink waiting to be used for urine samples. Nándor wore a kipah to consult and a short-sleeved shirt with braces; certainly in his most senior years those braces were a wardrobe feature.

George's mother's family had journeyed from Paris during World War II and back again after the war. That is where János went after the war, sometime between 1945 and 1949. His mother's parents rented a grand apartment near the Arc de Triomphe. His father had also worked for the Jewish welfare organisation, JDC, in Paris, as had Nándor during the war years in Budapest. Something else the two men could have talked about.

In Australia the family lived in a rent-controlled three-bedroom apartment at 2 Manion Avenue Rose Bay, where, as was the practice, they had to pay 'key money' for the rental but the rent-controlled aspect would have been a feature that enabled immigrants to live in an apartment home for several decades or more. George moved out of Manion Street at the age of 21.

He describes his backyard as the Cranbrook School oval, a generous playground for a young boy. The views across to the water take in the breathtaking beauty of Sydney. The family owned a dry-cleaning shop not too far away from their home. It was managed by his uncles and his mother and George occasionally worked there on Saturdays.

He describes his father as having impeccable honesty and unshakeable principles as he manoeuvred his way through working with key people in the community, including some difficult periods, marked by several years of unemployment.

While his parents did not have a wide circle of friends and his father didn't talk much about anything, the revelations about his past were somewhat more surprising.

Was it shyness, humility, or perhaps denial that one had played an important part in the war? Or was it just, 'Let's not talk about the war so as not to upset the children'? Or it may have been a manifestation of a more psychologically complex phenomenon of blocking out, wishing to forget the trauma of the past so as not to revisit and relive it? And then there is survivor guilt as everyone knew many who had not survived.

There are well-recorded personal memoirs where third-generation survivors revisit their grandparents' history, as in the 2023 French novel by Ann Berest, *The Postcard*, where the survivors get together, each with a number tattooed on their wrist or arm, to spend an evening together. There is some unspoken agreement that no one talks about their wartime experiences. They are living in the here and now, sometimes breaking into dance on their loungeroom floors. Their past experiences recede in the silence, and the music plays on; they sing and dance and flirt with each other as if there is no past or future—just the present to be savoured and enjoyed.

There is also the possibility that, as in my home, in Nándor's and in George's, there was the aforementioned publication, *Új Kelet* that appeared on the kitchen bench on a regular basis. The Hungarian language newspaper, first published in Kolozsvár (now Cluj-Napca) in 1918 and shut down in 1940, had recommenced publication in Tel Aviv, Israel, in 1948 as a weekly periodical. It soon re-emerged around the world for Hungarian speakers. It was a regular feature in many Hungarian-speaking households, well before the appearance of the World Wide Web, the internet, and social networks. *Új Kelet* transmitted information in pre-war and post-war years to Hungarian speakers and was the messenger to the Hungarian communities, wherever they were. It was a household name in many Sydney homes like mine, Nándor's and János Farkas' parents' home, or as George remembers, in his grandparents' home.

In the years 1948 till my departure from Sydney in 1966, this newspaper was to be found in every Hungarian Jewish household that I visited. It was the source of information and the stimulus for adult conversations. I did not attend school in Hungary or read in Hungarian, so it was only the masthead that I noticed and remember so vividly. I paid no attention to the content.

I grew up with *Új Kelet* at the time that it reported the notorious two-year-long Kasztner trial in detail as it took place in Israel in the 1950s. Its editor and Kasztner's boss was Ernő Márton, another key player in the Tel Aviv era when Kasztner was put under years of legal scrutiny during the politically strained postwar period in Israel.

The paper was an integral part of Rezső Kasztner's life. He began his journalistic career at the newspaper in Kolozsvár whilst studying law. When the paper ceased publication, Kasztner himself moved to Budapest to work with refugees. As the paper reemerged in Tel Aviv as a weekly from 1948, Kasztner once again joined the staff.

Új Kelet was a thread binding the Hungarian diaspora to the old country, now irrevocably wounded by war and genocide, as well as the new home of Israel, where survivors of the Holocaust were rebuilding their lives.

It followed news of importance to both the Hungarian and Israeli communities and was the spark for many debates in Hungarian households in Sydney. As it must have been, in March 1957, when it would have carried news of the ambush and assassination of Kasztner by Israeli extremists in Tel Aviv.

Chapter 10
Death of Kasztner and the Birth of Israel

As the Holocaust swept through Europe, many Jews in surrounding countries sought refuge in Budapest. That is where Kasztner was working with the Jewish Aid and Rescue Committee of Budapest, to support refugees, and where he developed his plan to buy passages on what was later labelled 'Kasztner's Train'.

There were attempts not only to provide refugees with food and shelter but also to furnish those who wanted with a visa to enter Palestine (now known as Israel). There were many who wanted to make the move, but at that time in the early 1940s, Palestine was under British rule and there were limits on those who could enter the British-ruled territory. Boats were turned back. There were horror stories, such as the time the 980-passenger ship, *St Louis,* was forced to return to Nazi-occupied Europe. Others drowned in the ocean as their ships capsized or were deliberately sunk. Thousands of Jewish refugees trying to enter what later became the State of Israel were caught and transferred to British prison camps in the desert islands of Cyprus or Mauritius. They lived there for months and years, in primitive tents without running water or electricity, enduring extremes of heat and cold.

Men like Carl Lutz at the Swiss Embassy and Raoul Wallenberg at the Swedish Embassy were working with hundreds of young Zionists and volunteers to produce the exit passes for families, often through Romania. But those who wanted to enter Israel had another hurdle to cross, which included access to the British-held protectorate. Despite the obstacles, many managed to do that, as thousands of European survivors landed in Israel every day. By 1948 there were 350,000 Holocaust survivors in Palestine.

In Palestine there was not much sympathy for them. The Jewish population were doing it tough, dealing with the hazards of the land, their hostile neighbours, and by 1947, they were militantly fighting the British.

***

The Kasztners moved to Palestine in late 1947, towards the end of the first phase of the War of Independence which continued into the following year. A lot was happening there, and Rezső was not greeted with any fanfare, contrary to his own expectation that he would be hailed as a hero.

Yoel Palgi, previously known as Emil Nussbacher,[1] was one of the three parachutists, along with Peretz Goldstein and Hannah Szenes, who were considered to be heroes in Israel. Palgi had written a runaway bestseller in 1946 titled *Behold a Great Wind Came,* where he praised Kasztner for his leadership of the Aid and Rescue Committee. He considered Kasztner 'brilliant and fearless in his handling of the negotiations in Hungary' although he had not been able to save the parachutists' mission to rescue Jews in Hungary. Palgi himself survived by jumping out of a train that was to take the captured parachutists to an internment camp, but the other two were not so fortunate.

Palgi wrote a 'warm, welcoming article' in one of the local papers describing Kasztner as a man who had risked his life so that others could live.

Kasztner got a job at *Új Kelet*, which was considered at that time to be a small circulation Hungarian language newspaper where he had worked previously in Kolozsvár. The publisher Ernő Márton had been his boss before Rezső left for Budapest in spring 1941, and was with him again in Tel Aviv. He was commissioned to create Hungarian-language radio and was considered to be an engaging, witty interviewer.

In April 1948, Israel established a new leftist Mapai government led by David Ben Gurion. Kasztner had political aspirations and saw opportunity.

In January 1949, Kasztner decided to run as a Mapai candidate but was placed 59th on the Party's slate. He had no chance of being elected. He tried again in 1951 and was 53rd on the slate. He was not elected that time either, but in 1951 he was appointed head of Public Relations in the Ministry of Commerce.

He continued to write for *Új Kelet* and was considered by some to be '... confident to the point of arrogance'.

Tommy Lapid—Kasztner's former colleague at *Új Kelet* and former member of the Knesset (Hebrew for Assembly, the parliament) described him as 'quick-witted, sarcastic, smarter than anyone else, and happy to show off in front of the less well-endowed'.

Things started to unravel for Kasztner who discovered that Moshe Krausz had filed a complaint with the Jewish Agency Executive and the Zionist Congress claiming that Kasztner had been 'pointlessly hobnobbing' with the Nazis while he, Krausz, had worked hard to save thousands in Protected Houses. He blamed Kasztner for failing to get exit visas for those with immigration certificates to Palestine. He was suspicious of Kasztner's friendship with the Nazi Kurt Becher, who had become Kasztner's preferred negotiator when dealing with Eichmann and considered him to be a 'megalomaniac' focused on his personal glory. Indeed, Kasztner famously testified in favour of Becher in the postwar trials in Nuremberg which helped Becher to avoid prosecution and to live till his mid-80s in Germany.

Kasztner wanted to clear his name with the Jewish Agency in Geneva. But things just got worse.

Then, in August 1952, Malchiel Grünwald, an elderly pamphleteer and stamp collector who owned a seedy hotel in downtown Jerusalem, made a personal attack against Kasztner. Grünwald had lost his son in the 1948 Arab–Israeli war, and some family in the Holocaust. He was characterised as an angry, disappointed man who had wanted to be a journalist. The brash, power-hungry, conflicted hero of the Holocaust, Kasztner, now a public figure, seemed to provoke his outrage. He published a mimeographed document, *Letters to the Friends of Mizrachi,* a conservative religious Zionist group that Krausz would have been part of.

He wrote '... I smell rotting carrion ... Kasztner has to be finished off ... Dr R. Kasztner must be liquidated.' He accused Kasztner of 'saving 52 members of his own family at the expense of thousands he had left to die.' He accused Ben Gurion's Labour Party of complicity in these actions.

Initially, Kasztner wanted to ignore the 'rants' but was encouraged to defend himself. The government wanted to sue Grünwald for 'malicious libel'. Kasztner's friend Hansi Brand believes that he gave in to persistent urging by Chaim Cohen, the Public Prosecutor and Attorney General, because 'He had always loved the limelight. He had grown used to it in Hungary and later in Austria. ... He craved recognition.'

Grünwald was represented by Shmuel Tamir, a 30-year-old, born in Jerusalem, and a graduate of the Hebrew University Law Faculty. An eloquent speaker and passionate opponent of Mapai, the Labour Party, Tamir was a member of the right-wing revisionists as one of the founders of Herut (Freedom Party).

He regarded Ben Gurion's negotiations with the British on a par with Kasztner's with the Nazis. The trial opened on 1 January, 1954. A sole judge was appointed. There was no jury system.

Kasztner testified for three weeks. He was overly confident and nonchalantly suggested to Tamir that when all this is over, they get together as two lawyers—'to compare notes over a glass of wine'.

Tamir was not taken in. He was ambitious and somewhat ruthless, as prosecutors can be. He accused Kasztner of withholding information from the Jews of Hungary about the Vrba and Wetzler report that had come from Auschwitz.

It was no longer a simple libel action but: *The Kasztner Trial*.

The Attorney General had initially appointed an inexperienced lawyer, Amnon Tel, as Assistant Attorney for the Jerusalem District to represent the prosecution to run the case. But as the trial dragged on, at the five-month mark, Chaim Cohen, the Public Prosecutor, took over the prosecution, realising that more expertise was required.

It was now 1955 and the focus in Israel was on the elections. Not wanting the distraction, Kasztner withdrew his candidacy.

How can someone who never faced the Nazis judge those who did? That was the view held by Kasztner and other survivors who had direct dealings with the Nazis. Kasztner lost his job at the radio station. Judge Benjamin Halevi did not 'disappoint' the prosecutor, Shmuel Tamir. He came down with a harsh judgement against Kasztner.

In his judgement, Judge Halevi blamed the Hungarian Jewish leadership, particularly Kasztner, for not warning Hungarians that their journey on the trains would be their last, for not pushing them to escape and mount an armed resistance. For him: 'Kasztner had traded the lives of fellow Jews for lives of a privileged few'.

As part of the judgement in the trial, Judge Halevi, later a Herut (right-wing) member of the Knesset (parliament) wrote that the opportunity of rescuing prominent people appealed to him greatly. He considered '... the rescue of the most important Jews as a personal success and a success for Zionism'. It was success that would also justify his conduct—his political negotiation with Nazis and the Nazi patronage of his committee.

When Kasztner received this 'present' from the Nazis, 'Kasztner sold his soul to the German Satan.'

The Szatmár Rabbi of the ultrareligious Chassidim who was one of the passengers on the Kasztner train, was called to provide testimony. When asked whether it was Kasztner and his efforts that had saved him and the other Rabbis, he said, 'No,' presumably pointing to the heavens, 'it was the Almighty who had saved him and not Kasztner.'

Halevi accepted Krausz's testimony and blamed Kasztner for not working *with* Krausz but *against* him. Halevi said that Kasztner's testimony had exonerated Kurt Becher, knowing he was a war criminal, to justify his own actions.

He compared Kasztner to Faust who made a 'pact with the devil'. He said that 'Kasztner had sold his soul to the devil' in order to save a few. He did not agree that Kasztner had shared booty with Becher, so Grünwald was asked to pay for that bit of libel: one pound.

In the newspaper headlines, Kasztner was accused of being a Nazi collaborator, and perhaps the worst title an Israeli could be smeared with: 'Eichmann's partner'.

That day Kasztner made a statement to the media that he 'had fallen a victim of a terrible injustice' comparing himself to the Jewish French military officer, Alfred Dreyfus, who had been accused of treason in France in the late 1800s.[2]

Kasztner was going to clear his name. *The New York Times* ran a headline, 'Quisling Charge Stirs All Israel'.

For Kasztner, the period was one of unmitigated horror. He stayed at the office till late and went home after dark.

The government indicated it would appeal the case and challenge the finding. It was considered to be too big an issue for one judge to decide.

Prime Minister Ben Gurion said, 'Those who were safe during the Hitler era ought not to presume to judge their brethren who were burned and slaughtered, nor the few who survived.'

Many would argue that to be told how Jews should behave in 1944 by those who were not there was not acceptable.

The Government's appeal was filed on 21 August. There was little public appetite for Kasztner's defence. Israelis didn't want to discuss the Holocaust, much less have the facts of its survival litigated in public. The mood in the newly established country was in many senses euphoric, but there were harsh realities. Whilst they were absorbing immigrants, building their new identity, evolving their modern Hebrew language, they were also fighting insurgents from their Arab neighbours.

In March 1956, the perjury charge was dismissed, and Israel quickly moved on. On 29 October 1956, the Israeli army invaded Egypt and occupied the Sinai Peninsula, and the Kasztner court case was not the most critical issue for the media.

Kasztner continued to work for *Új Kelet*. He was receiving many abusive, threatening calls, so took to not answering the phone. In the aftermath of his public disgrace, he rang his daughter to say that 'he had done his best and that he was a mensch'[3] which translates from the Yiddish language as 'a good human being'. Being a mensch is a Yiddish phrase that is proudly used to describe a person who has led a good and decent life. Often, the best single-word description that can be put on a gravestone.

On 3 March 1957, after the court case had concluded, Kasztner was working late at the office and drove his long-time boss, Ernő Márton, home. He parked his car in front of 6 Sderot Emanuel Street, a typical inner urban apartment that lines Tel Aviv streets. Today, cars are tightly parked along the street, but as fewer people had cars in the 1950s, the cars would have been more sparsely lined up. While still in the driver's seat Kasztner was approached by two men. He saw a third standing in the shadows of the building.

One man, Ze'ev Eckstein, asked if he was Kasztner. When he said 'Yes,' the man pulled a pistol and took aim. It misfired, or according to Eckstein in the 2008 documentary, *Killing Kasztner*, the barrel had no ammunition—Kasztner got out of the car, pushed him aside and ran toward the entrance of the building. The assassin fired again—fired two shots, and a further one came from the assailants in the parked car; this time the bullets found their target. Kasztner ran a few more steps and collapsed. The three assailants fled. Kasztner died on 15 March at 7.20 am.

Új Kelet published a moving obituary written by Ernő Márton which praised Kasztner for 'wit and erudition' and his efforts in saving the lives of Jews. The obituary celebrated his 'death-defying courage and self-sacrifice and his ambition to do something great, something eternally significant' for his people. (*Új Kelet*, 17 April,1957)

Ze'ev Eckstein was a right-wing extremist who, after the ambush outside Kasztner's apartment on the fateful evening of 3 March and Kasztner's subsequent death in hospital, claimed he was avenging the death of Jews in Europe. It is considered that Kasztner became the first victim of a Jewish assassination in the State of Israel.

For all the praise that Kasztner had received in obituaries and judgements as he cleared his name, his larger-than-life and less-than-perfect personality seemed to have contributed both to his success as a negotiator, brave taker of risks in the service of others, quick wit, and sharp tongue. As gifted as he was in ability, he raised the ire of some to the point where he himself was a casualty of war.

As his friend Hansi Brand, who was his companion in Budapest in the midst of his negotiations with Eichmann, and with whom he continued to be close in Israel, said: 'I think the most important thing was not to be a hero but to survive'. As close as she was to Kasztner, was that statement her summation of his personality? That could also have been the message that Eichel and Farkas carried silently in their heads.

On 7 January 1958, three men were convicted of murder and sentenced to life imprisonment. A week later, the Supreme Court 4:1 exonerated Rezső Kasztner. Justice Shimon Agranot concluded that Judge Halevi had acted from hindsight. It was too late for Kasztner to celebrate. The men were released after six years.

How the trial played out and the recriminations that followed led some to characterise the two main antagonists in the affair: Grünwald the pamphleteer who had brought the case as the bullet, and Krausz, who had testified against Kasztner as the gun.[4] The relationship between Krausz and Kasztner was never good, and only grew more poisonous until its fatal conclusion.

There were also political repercussions with the Mapai Party losing five seats to Herut at the elections.

There was a historical irony. Tamir, the lawyer who ran the case against Kasztner faced a Kasztnerian dilemma of his own late in life when, in May 1985, he represented Minister of Defence, Yitzhak Rabin, in negotiations to release Israeli prisoners from Lebanon and he negotiated 1,100 terrorists for only three Israeli soldiers. The Israeli commentariat judged him bitterly. The families of the three soldiers felt differently.

She came my way

One of the witnesses who testified in Kasztner's trial was Kati Szenes, mother of the third parachutist, Hannah Szenes, who had not survived and was treated as a heroine with the grandest funeral that Israel had seen at the time when her body was returned to Israel for burial in 1950. Her funeral contrasted to that of Kasztner's more modest burial. Hannah had been arrested in Budapest in June 1944. When her mother found out about her imprisonment (where there was torture and interrogation), she engaged in a desperate attempt to help release her daughter.

During the trial, Kati Szenes claimed that she went to Hungarian Police, prison officers, lawyers' chambers, government offices and the Síp Street offices of the Rescue Committee for help, and Kasztner would not see her. Nándor's family recalled a conversation when Nándor Eichel mentioned to his adult children that 'Kati Szenes went through my hands'. But we do not have more detail. He clearly didn't want to say more, but let it be known that he was working in those circles, particularly with the police and as a welfare worker who visited prisons.

What it implies is that Nándor and others were well aware of the Kasztner trial as they read their *Új Kelet* and were likely to drop such comments in conversation at the time. It is also very likely that Nándor had worked with Lutz and Krausz as well as Kasztner. At least they had also come his way. He would most likely have had a lot to do with the offices of the Aid and Rescue Committee, led by Kasztner.

Kasztner was a Zionist, and now his granddaughter, Merav Michaeli, has held a strong leadership role in Israeli politics. Merav, an Israeli television personality and journalist, became a member of the Israeli Knesset in 2013 and subsequently the head of the Labour Party. The 2008 documentary film by Gaylen Ross, *Killing Kasztner*, tells the story of the assassination and brings together the lead assassin, Ze'ev Eckstein, with Kasztner's family, including granddaughter Merav. She describes that when she and her mother Zsuzsi met with her grandfather's killer, she, Merav, felt as if in a 'coma'. For her mother, it was cathartic; Ze'ev was reflective and acknowledged his responsibility. The movie was well-received in Israel. There is a generation who have not been brought up on the negative charges against Kasztner. It is now widely accepted that he was badly mistreated. Times have changed. Today Kasztner would have been proud of Merav.

As a parent or grandparent, one is proud of your children's achievements, but how much more so when you can feel the long game, unforeseen at the time, to be achieving what you would have wanted to accomplish. Merav has led the high-profile media and political life that Kasztner himself would have wanted to lead.

Kasztner and the Budapesti Schindlers helped in some way to do more than save lives. Did the lives that Kasztner and the Budapesti Schindlers saved make a new, more hopeful generation possible? There's that famous line that wartime resistance means burning your future to make possible a better future that you will never see.

There is another modest plaque at 8 Váci Street where Kasztner rented apartments in 1941:[5]

DR REZSŐ KASZTNER (1906–1957)
DURING THE HOLOCAUST AS A MEMBER OF THE
BUDAPEST RESCUE COMMITTEE, HE RISKED HIS OWN LIFE
TO SAVE THE LIFE OF MANY OTHERS.
ERECTED BY THE KASZTNER MEMORIAL COMMITTEE 1998.

Új Kelet: The Messenger

In January 2024 I met Sydney man, Danny Avidan, the nephew of Rosie Gluck. He was keen to talk about Nándor Eichel: their family doctor, friend and hero. I also listened to his mother, Susan Avidan's 1995 testimonial held in the Spielberg archives. The testimonial, backed up by Danny's recollections, reports that Danny's grandmother, Clara, and mother, Susan, along with her sisters and cousins, were saved by Nándor Eichel.

In 1944, Danny's grandmother had a brother in Sweden. Just at the time Raoul Wallenberg was heading to Budapest, a mission he was keen to do as he had strong links there through his Hungarian business partner. Wallenberg had been given a list of family names for whom he arranged documents through the Swedish Red Cross as a document of protection, before the Schutzpasses came into being.

This enabled the grandparents and other family members to move into Swedish safe houses and work with Wallenberg in Budapest in the turbulent months of 1944-1945. The grandparents enjoyed relative freedom of movement and were not required to wear the yellow star whilst working within the Swedish diplomatic sphere, and assisted in the task of writing exit certificates for the Embassy.

Meanwhile, things were not going well in Budapest, and those who had contacts or money did everything they could to secure their safety. Young family members were encouraged to leave Budapest, including Susan, Rosie and her cousins. They were able to secure some family protection by arranging through a female contact for their daughters and nieces to receive new Christian identities, which most likely were those of that woman's own nieces and nephews. They went with new names on birth certificates as they settled into the farming community of Kiskunhalas, 130 kilometres south of Budapest. Their various hideouts were raided numerous times by the gendarmes. The group had to be rescued each time and then relocated. When the grandparents heard that they had been apprehended it was Nándor who rescued them, by bringing Swedish papers arranged by the grandparents to get them released.

On one occasion Nándor boarded a train carriage and pulled one of the girls, either Rosie or Susan, off the train and away from the terrible fate that most likely would have awaited them. Nándor reassured her, 'It will be all right.' In the family's telling, Nándor was wearing the Gestapo uniform as a disguise. That must have been a uniquely daring feat even in wartime. Wallenberg was known to have had access to some of those uniforms for rescue purposes, so who got the uniforms and who wore them remains a mystery. Whoever did, these were bold and brave acts in desperate times. It is very likely that Nándor, too, was working with Wallenberg, or at least the Swedish Embassy.

In July 1944, the women, along with several children as part of their group, were in Szarvas. The gendarmes arrived in the village and interrogated one sister, Margit, who, when questioned, denied that she was Jewish, and for that she was put on a train that went straight to Auschwitz, never to return. The rest of the group was taken captive.

That was another time that Nándor came to the rescue.

Nándor found the sisters and the cousins in a Budapest jail when they were put into a holding room with people who were converts to Judaism. Nándor came to the jail delivering 'kosher food' and whilst the deliveries were not for Susan and her cousin, she tried to get to him as the family knew him well from Budapest. Like Nándor, the grandfather was an Orthodox Rabbi. The two men had most likely worshipped in the same Orthodox Synagogue in Kazinczy Street.

When the women could finally get access to Nándor, he instantly recognised them, asking why they had not told him of their whereabouts sooner. He was clearly a close family friend and rescuer. Nándor went straight to the Swedish Embassy and arranged to have them released. Their mother Clara arrived with an 'amazing basket of food'. An important part of a mother's rescue mission!

On 15 October 1944, when the Arrow Cross came to power, they would go into the so-called Swedish 'safe houses' and take people to the Danube. Once more, the family group went into hiding. This time to Nagymaros, again with false papers. Money was running out, but the young members of the family stayed together. Susan commented in her testimonial that 'it was just a matter of luck who stayed alive and who did not'. But somehow the family had luck and resources, including the help of Nándor, to be able to survive both in Budapest and outside.

Danny remembers his mother, Susan, describing Nándor as a 'saint'. His mother 'thought the world' of Nándor. Susan's sister Rosie Gluck is one person who remembers being saved by Nándor Eichel.

It seems that Nándor was working both with the Swedish and Swiss Embassies as a representative of the Jewish communities. Wallenberg was certainly in the picture. But Nándor was also likely to be working with Lutz, Kasztner and Krausz, getting Palestinian visas for exit. It was to Palestine that Susan and her family went after the war.

The likelihood is that Nándor was working in some way with all these Budapesti Schindlers and indeed could be described as one himself.

Susan married in Israel in 1950 and came to Australia in 1967, where the family lived a 'very happy life'. When it was time to ask Susan about the past, whether it was Danny or the grandchildren wanting to explore their roots, she would say, 'We don't talk about that. Let's talk about happy times in Israel and Australia.' The 'sad' past seemed beyond limits.

Danny considers Nándor and his wife Pesza as extended family. They spent many Jewish holiday celebratory meals together. When Danny landed in Australia, Pesza taught him English in her home, where he went after school, somewhat reluctantly as an 11-year-old. When the family visited Nándor's surgery in Bellevue Hill, Nándor would not let them pay for the consultations. Nándor drove Danny in his Holden car to the soccer. By then, his son Robert was studying medicine, so Nándor had someone to induct into the sport. It was known within the family that they owed their survival to Nándor, so when Danny, as an adult, struck up the courage to ask Nándor about his war experiences, Nándor responded, 'We don't talk about that.' Thus, the cone of silence was continued in all quarters.

***

As previously noted, *Új Kelet* was a feature in all our homes, mine, Nándor's, Danny's and that of George Farkas.

Új Kelet was the source of information for Jewish Hungarians around the world, most clearly so in Sydney, Australia, where it must have been readily available in the local shops of Bondi, Rose Bay and Double Bay. The newspaper has its own unique story of survival, from inception in Kolozsvár, closure in the 1940s, rebirth in postwar Israel and return to Cluj-Napoca.

The history of *Új Kelet* reflects the need of shattered communities of the scattered Hungarian Jews to remain connected. It seems to have always been there, so it took me back to *Nefelejcs utca, Do Not Forget Me Street,* a street that will not let itself be forgotten.

Between the years 2015 and 2019 the newspaper was published monthly, and since 2019 it has been published quarterly. Once again, it has offices located in Cluj-Napoca, Romania, and is published in Tel Aviv today under the artistic directorship of a gay rights activist and blogger, Israeli media personality, Kristof Steiner.

I certainly knew my uncle Nándor, but not in the way I wanted to. I went on this family journey to attempt to walk in his shoes and join others like him so that I could better understand the times, the dilemmas of doing rescue work in Budapest in 1944. But as the famous philosopher Martin Buber[6] has cautioned, it is not possible to walk entirely in another's shoes—despite our best efforts. Yet I certainly tried to do just that to the best of my ability, so as not to forget him or his peers in save and rescue work, and the Budapest of 1944-1945 with the street that doesn't want to be forgotten.

Part 4

*'Be silent as to services you have rendered
but speak of favours you have received.'*

—Epictetus

Chapter 11
Philosophy, psychology and silence

On a fine September afternoon in 2023, I ventured into the magnificent Baillieu Library at the University of Melbourne, which I had not visited for a number of years. After all, these days most research is done online through access to electronic journals, particularly in my field of psychology, where the most recent publications are of interest rather than the historic tomes. Here I was going up the spiral staircase to the third floor of a library that was fast becoming transformed into a place of quiet refuge for students on their laptops rather than those in search of a book. I was taking in this contemporary library landscape with curiosity and keen expectations as I eagerly anticipated what I might find, and what I might learn, on the shelves holding books numbered 323.1192 on Floor 3.

Having been alerted to the reference about Nándor Eichel in Randolph Braham's book by my colleagues at the Memorial Museum of Hungarian-Speaking Jewry in Israel, I was keen to explore what more I could learn from the two-volume, 1,200+ pages of the English language, *The Politics of Genocide*. And here it was; the volumes could be found in Holocaust museums that I searched, and on the shelves of my very own University's library.

I located the heavy volumes and lifted them both down by standing on the bottom shelf. It was clear that Nándor's name was there, but so were thousands of other names and notes regarding those turbulent years in Hungary that I was interested in. Every town and geographic location was listed. Interspersed with the detailed recording of people, dates, and events was commentary and personal observations made by the man who had not only written these tomes, but who had also written many others on the topic that he knew well.

Randolph Braham was as interesting as the subjects he wrote about. Born into a Hungarian Jewish family in Bucharest, Romania, in 1922, he had lived through the events that he was recording and writing about, a working scholar till the very last days of his life. He died in Queens, New York City, USA, in 2018. He was born Adolph Abraham but chose to change his name to Randolph L. Braham. Indeed, it was very much as if he was shedding his confusing Holocaust coat in his name and donning a different Anglicised one for the recording of history.

...

Randolph Braham, working as an academic in the United States, having changed his name when recording history, did not hide his identity, but neither did he declare it. In his magnum opus, *The Politics of Genocide,* he did use as a photo illustration—perhaps the only one without a source reference—a photograph of his own dog tag. He did reveal himself as a Holocaust survivor. In 2011 he was recognised by the Hungarian Government for his body of research, but in 2014 he famously returned his medals and resigned from The Order of Merit of the Republic of Hungary and refused the use of his name in connection with Holocaust Memorial Centre, after excessive government interference in 2014, because he felt that the country had white-washed the Holocaust.

Professor Braham was outraged at the time by what he described as attempts by Hungary's then current nationalist government to equate the murder of nearly 600,000 Jews in Hungary with the suffering of other Hungarians under the German occupation—'a German occupation, as the record clearly shows, that was not only unopposed but generally applauded' by the country's wartime regime, he wrote. Times have changed and Victor Orban's current government (2025) takes a different view.[1]

Braham also asked that his name be removed from the Library and Information Centre of the Holocaust Memorial Centre, or *Holokauszt Emlékközpont*, in Budapest.

'I realize that for a variety of political and economic reasons the leaders responsible for the operation of the *Holokauszt Emlékközpont* would or could not speak out against the brazen drive to falsify history', he wrote to the president of the Centre. 'I, on the other hand, a survivor whose parents and many family members were among the hundreds of thousands of murdered Jews, cannot remain silent, especially since it was my destiny to work on the preservation of the historical record of the Holocaust.'

With or without his disclosure, his work is hugely significant and has been described as an 'immensely precise, panoramic and microscopic study of the Hungarian Holocaust.'

His lack of disclosure stands in stark contrast to a man like Kasztner, whose ambition and desire for recognition are likely to have contributed to his downfall. Why would Braham maintain his silence about his identity and eschew the unique authority and credibility that his life experience conferred?

Additionally, Braham must have in some respects been personally driven to make his life's work the recording of the critical years in Budapest in numerous volumes, including his *Politics of Genocide*. In that sense, by first not disclosing, he may consciously have wished others not to define him by his past, but ultimately, when returning the award, his voice was loud and strong.

Did he cultivate another form of silence—as when the researcher does not want their research to be judged as tainted by whatever the reader might conjecture, such as lack of objectivity, driven by emotion, or blind to the facts? The reader can then accept the data and the historical records as evidence of what occurred, without judging the researcher. Is this another type of silence?

Silence can be a cloak against credit—and the right *not* to be judged as biased in the role of an academic, a recorder of Budapesti history. Staying objective as a recorder of events one may or may not have experienced is a human challenge. Readers make their own judgement, consciously or otherwise.

Whatever the motivation to stay silent about his past, at least for much of his academic career, Professor Braham conducted that work over three decades, from 1962, when City College hired him to be a lecturer, until 1992, when he retired as their distinguished professor of political science. He founded the Rosenthal Institute in 1979 and continued to serve as its director.

How history is recorded and accepted is of utmost importance. None of us was there as witness to events, but today there are many who may wish to deny the facts. Since facts are known to some, but not to all, there needs to be forensic research in the bookshelves of reputable libraries, or access to records such as personal testimonies, so the clearest light can be shone brightly on the past.

Then there is the wish to stay silent because the facts speak for themselves, and the researcher does not want to take credit for the events as a mere recorder. One wants to be out of the picture and out of view, to adopt the impersonal, scientific silence of the microscope, the pen and paper. In this way, we expect that the audience will judge and make sense of events for themselves.

The writer is not seeking credit or personal significance; they want the written word or text to do the job. As an academic, I am too familiar with the need to remain unbiased, and also to be seen as such. And as a psychologist, I want to understand the other, be aware of my personal biases where they exist, and to learn to put them aside.

The dignity of silence: Braham-Eichel-Farkas

There is also the dignity of silence. You leave the past behind, never looking back, and doggedly pursue a different life with new careers, focus on family, and what today we would call wellbeing. Just 'getting on with it', to use the classic British idiom, and not reliving or revisiting the past. The past contributes to who we are, the sum total of our experiences; we need not deny it, but at the same time, it need not define how we deal with the present.

Eichel and Farkas chose to live their lives in Sydney without casting the shadow of the Holocaust over their family experiences. They lived their lives as respected members of the Sydney community. They did not seek recognition, or benefit, or try to influence others, but never hid from the facts when approached (except when I visited Nándor with tape recorder in hand, or the chronicler of the Spielberg Archives approached him). Clearly, he did not wish his testimony to be on record so as not to be judged, lauded or critiqued. Those of us who were not there, or too young to remember, would not be in a position to judge. And as the first-hand witnesses no longer have a voice, the descendants may not be in the best position to opine.

Jews rescuing Jews

There is another factor that may account for the silence of the Budapesti Schindlers: the tendency for Jews who performed feats of heroism for their own people to be more likely to be excluded from the narrative, as a matter of historical recording.

During my quest for information about Nándor's wartime activities, and the visit to the Memorial Museum of Hungarian Speaking Jewry in Safed, I naively queried the fact that so many Righteous among the Nations had been recognised by Yad Vashem since 1953, when the State of Israel enacted the Holocaust and Remembrance Law. In doing so, the State entrusted Yad Vashem with the responsibility of commemorating the Righteous Among the Nations, a recognition given to non-Jews who risked their lives to save Jews during the Holocaust. These were men like Schindler, Lutz, and Wallenberg. But I knew of no such recognition being awarded to heroic Jews.

I was directed to Yuval Alpan of the *Committee to Recognise the Heroism of Jewish Rescuers During the Holocaus*t, who made me aware of the progress that had been made in that regard.

It is very much the case that there were collaborations between Jews and non-Jewish rescuers. In fact, when Lutz was recognised by the Jewish National Fund for his rescue work, he pointed to Krausz as the one who should have received the credit.

Eichel and Farkas sit right within that category, Eichel working with Lutz and most likely with Wallenberg and others; while Farkas worked with Wallenberg. Neither sought recognition, and the time for that might well have passed. Their silence after eight decades has not helped provide the documentation that records their deeds.

The rescue of one Jew by another Jew has been taken for granted as an obligation. All Jews have a responsibility for each other, which is expressed in different ways, such as the timeless Jewish edict, 'Neither shalt thou stand idly by the blood of thy neighbour' *Leviticus 19:16*. At other times it is expressed as, 'He who saves a life saves the world'. In 2011, the *Jewish Rescuer's Citation* was established by the Committee in partnership with the Bnei Brith World Centre, with 617 people receiving the citation to date. Of them, 340 have been awarded to Hungarians, whilst the remainder were given to heroes from France, Greece, Germany, Slovakia, Russia, Belarus, Ukraine, Yugoslavia, Lithuania, Poland, Italy, Belgium, Romania, Morocco, the Netherlands, and numerous other communities.

Krausz and Kasztner have, to date, not received that recognition because they are deemed to be 'controversial figures', not universally applauded. However, when I read Braham's recording of events, they both seemed entirely worthy. Braham ascribes Krausz a great deal of credit, while Porter's Kasztner is critical of Krausz as she describes that '... they clearly didn't get on'. But Porter weighs down on the merits and exceptional capabilities and dedication of Kasztner to saving the lives of as many as he could. As Nándor Eichel said to his daughter about Kasztner, 'He just did what he could.' And the controversy rages on, seven-plus decades later.

Long silences

There are many reasons why adults stay silent. I recall a heavy silence in the family home on some nights during our time as refugees in France. Clearly there were tensions in our parents' relationship when they were living in two hotel rooms in Paris, cooking for a family of five on a single-burner kerosene stove, destination unknown, with two, perhaps three suitcases and a baby to contend with.

The trauma of those postwar years and the earlier relentless, omnipresent fear of Nazi occupation and the acute trauma of facing the Arrow Cross death squad, believing that one's last moments would be on the banks of the Danube, would have taken its toll on my father.

And there must have been some emotion when leaving the 'Paris of the East'—the language they knew so well, and the fact of saying goodbye to family that they loved, not knowing whether they would ever see each other again. To borrow a truism (with apologies from Tolstoy): all Holocaust survivors have trauma, but each is traumatised in their own way.

Each carries with them a complex array of experiences and emotions all locked into that bucket of emotion that, for some, surfaces as anger; and for others, like my family, lands in silence.

But regret about what is left behind, anxiety about the future and anger about what might be occurring in the present are all valid emotions under the circumstances. The manifestations of anger are many, both physical and verbal; the damage is often long-term and irreversible.

Anger can be a most powerful emotion that can be harnessed to deal with danger rather than the human 'fight or flight' response, such as when the sabre-toothed tiger approached our ancestors in the wild. Amassing one's resources cognitively and emotionally, that is, keeping one's cool under extreme stress, such as when dealing with Nazis or the Fascists, must have served the Budapesti Schindlers well. They would have used their anger to propel them into action rather than jeopardising outcomes. Psychologists such as the late Charles Spielberger have written extensively about the health implications of keeping one's anger under check rather than letting it out, better known as 'anger in', as a form of suppression, and 'anger out' as anger directed towards another, or the external environment. There is a price to pay if one is not aware of the emotion and the conscious choices one makes to manage his or her anger. Clearly these two forms of anger apply differently in different circumstances. Regardless, there is a cost for both losing one's cool *or* suppressing one's anger.

So, when it comes to the post-Holocaust era, when people are dealing with the remnants of their everyday lives, suppressed anger may be quite costly. In contrast, silence is often labelled as passive aggression; those silences when one holds back and dares not articulate what is on one's mind. I certainly saw our mother stressed, weighed down by the burden of keeping a belt manufacturing operation in the kitchen, supporting an ailing husband no more than 50 years old, and three daughters who were adapting to a new life of freedom much faster than their parents were. I reflect on how my parents dealt with anger.

During my Australian childhood, many Hungarian migrants in Sydney worked in the clothing trade and owned factories in Oxford Street. Belts were needed for the waisted garments that women wore in the 1950s, so the belt factory was born in the kitchen of our flat. Little investment in machinery was required; mainly hand-held hole punchers and various types of staplers were used.

My mother collected fabric from three or four Oxford Street factories and delivered it to various neighbourhood outworkers, including the lady downstairs with the heavy-drinking husband. The outworkers sewed the belts and then they were finished off in our kitchen factory before being packaged for delivery to Oxford Street. My mother did all the deliveries by tram, and when I was old enough, I did that too. My father punched the holes into the belts at a small kitchen bench where he could remain seated and have a smoke or two.

As children we were certainly integrating rapidly into the Australian lifestyle at Bondi Beach, something neither parent was prepared for. We joined our friends at the beach wearing what would have been considered by our parents as 'daring' swimsuits, eating forbidden foods, and being caught with boys, whether they were neighbourhood friends or our teenage companions.

There were frayed tempers and many angry outbursts as our parents tried to bring us into line.

There is general agreement that when there is anger, it is helpful to bring it to the surface and express what it is. In our household it was not the hard work or the health trauma that had to be dealt with, as Nándor was always on hand to help, but rather the fear of the new, when familiar ways and practices that had helped the family survive for generations as Magyars, were slipping away. But the body keeps the score. Indeed, my father passed away at the age of 53 and my mother lived a decade or so longer, but also died at what one would now call a relatively young age: 63.

How one remembers a childhood, whether it is the smiles, the love, the trauma, or the burden of guilt carried by adults, is difficult to unravel. As a young child I did not think too much about these things but rather just kept playing with the children in the neighbourhood, enjoying school, friendships and leisure.

But for Nándor, and perhaps for my mother too, there was declared regret, some self-blame or guilt that more could not be done to save their sister, Rose. And perhaps for Nándor, guilt, self-blame or regret for the many that he *could not* save, or concern for the many he may not yet have known that he had saved. For my father, too, it was the loss of his sister Mati; something I never once heard him speak about.

And by war's end everyone knew of the countless losses all around—the uncle who had lost a wife and nine children, and one who had lost a wife and just two. The calculations of grief and sorrow defy understanding. No one was counting the losses; they knew the numbers. They were just annually lining up and lighting what we call the 24-hour memorial or 'Yarzait' candles, for each of their losses. The word literally means 'year-time' in Yiddish, and is the anniversary of the death of a loved one which is commemorated annually by observant Jews. Those who had not lost their faith followed this with a visit to the synagogue to say the traditional kaddish prayer. Additionally, they would visit on days such as Yom Kippur, the holiest day of the year, and on several other significant Jewish holidays when a part of the service known as Yizkor (or Remembrance in Hebrew) is dedicated to the memory of lost loved ones. Before the prayers are said, the children are asked to leave as the grown-ups weep and wail long and hard, as they experience the grief and loss once more. On those occasions, it is not the silence of childhood that one remembers, but a public outpouring of grief.

Family secrets

Families are renowned for holding 'family secrets'. Sometimes what is kept from children is of no consequence, and on other occasions it is *highly* significant. While many Jewish parents of my parents' generation spoke Yiddish, Hungarian Jews often had German as their second language. When my parents spoke German, they clearly did not want us children to understand, but to us that was of no consequence; we didn't need to know their secrets, and in the main we were not aware of their grief. We lived our lives as young people enjoying our freedoms.

My parents never spoke about the Holocaust. As children and teenagers, we lived in our own worlds. We were not particularly psychologically minded or 'tuned in' as one might say today. There was the parent world and the child and teenage worlds. We each had our own domains and interests. We saw our parents as immigrants who spoke with a strange accent, worked hard, and also wanted us to retain their values and practices. Nevertheless, they did not seem to look back. There was a code of silence. The conversations with other likeminded refugees did not seem to happen. And we did not ask.

There is a story in the Bible that we all knew from childhood: the story of a woman who turned into a pillar of salt, Lot's wife. It is a moral tale to discourage us from looking back. In the First Book of the *Old Testament, Genesis,* the family, Lot and his wife and daughters, flee the 'wicked' city of Sodom that is about to be destroyed. Two visiting angels warned the family to leave, but instructed them not to look back. But Mrs Lot ignored the instruction and was subsequently turned into a pillar of salt.

Having such a powerful parable in one's religious teaching would be a clear encouragement to move forward and not look back at what one has left behind and is missing, unless it is garlic, onions, or capsicum, so that one can start a new life without regrets. That is the climate I grew up in.

Survivor guilt

For some, when the nightmare of the war ended, the nightmare of surviving began. Nándor was forever haunted by the sister he could not save. When you win a race, do you think of how the others might feel? When you celebrate your successes, feast and enjoy the best of what life has to offer, do we think of others? How much more so when there is a loss of life, and one survives and the other(s) do not. That is the reality for so many survivors of war, trauma, and disaster.

Guilt, in a general sense, is a phenomenon written about widely. Sigmund Freud in the 19th century wrote about how one can blame and beat oneself up about what was done, or what was not done, and how bad events may have been able to be prevented. Generally, guilt is not a helpful emotion in that it is akin to what coping research describes as self-blame, or self-punishment. In contrast to guilt, taking responsibility for one's actions and rectifying a situation whenever that is possible is a more helpful positive act. Self-blame and self-criticism are the *least* helpful in terms of maintaining one's wellbeing. After all, one can never turn back time.

Coping, resilience and fortitude

The question that has preoccupied me during my years of professional practice and research has been: What factors help us both to survive, and to thrive, and achieve the best outcomes for a good life despite what that life dishes up?

For almost four decades I have sought to answer those questions.

Indeed, there are personality characteristics that explain the outstanding successes of some and the shortcomings of others. The numerous heroes who have prompted me to go on this journey to explore the past have each had personal qualities that explain much of their bravery and boldness in the face of extraordinary obstacles. By no means have any of them been perfect men. Their failings are clearly evident in any biography that one chooses to read, but their actions to save others and do good shine through strongly.

My initial interest in psychological research has been in how people cope. How people manage adversity and retain balance, emotional fortitude and dignity. Those coping skills can be learnt even if one is not born with a propensity to be positive, optimistic, or brave.

'Resilience' is now part of our everyday vernacular. Everyone wants to know what the magic potion is that makes us resilient. Is it inherent, acquired through our genetic make-up? Or acquired through our childhood experiences?

It is clear that there is no simple formula for being resilient in all situations. We can certainly reflect on our experiences and personal journeys, and those of others, to develop and blend that magic potion. Resilience is made up of the skills that we utilise to cope, whether it is inherent in our personalities to be positive, tackle challenges face on and see the good in people; or skills that are learnt to maximise our survival and contribute to our thriving and that of our communities.

Then there are role models: people who meet or have met life's challenges that inspire us. There are no better examples than those who have gone through the horrors of war and start anew, working towards goals for their new life. Many do that with determination, diligence, perseverance and with extraordinary success.

In my pursuit of understanding how we build strengths and capacity, and how to create wellbeing and contentment, I have focused on how people deal with their stresses; that is, how they manage, thrive and survive.

The Budapesti Schindlers coped with the extraordinary circumstances that confronted them. From my vantage point, *they* were truly extraordinary: what we would now consider to be not only resilient people but people with immense fortitude. Being strong and going the extra mile when circumstances demanded it. But in their own minds, in the moment, they may have been just doing what had to be done. That is how Eichel described the work of Kasztner, rather than judging him for his morally complex methods. He did what was best under the circumstances.

In plain language, fortitude means strength. It comes from the Latin word *forte*, meaning strong. Over the years, people have come to define fortitude as bravery in the face of adversity. Really, it means having the courage or the resources to cope with whatever life dishes up. It is about having the mental and emotional strength to face difficulty, adversity, danger, or temptation courageously, and to essentially think beyond the self, and consider the good of others.

What makes the concept so appealing is that we can associate it with our everyday experiences. Most of us can relate to strength and recovery. We can also relate to living the good life.

Professor Marc Brackett, from Yale University, when asked what fortitude meant to him, replied that the word fortitude encompasses values such as 'being a good person', 'doing the right thing', 'being upright' and being able to 'self-regulate'. These values, along with going beyond just doing the *right* thing but also doing *good*, are well accounted for in the philosophy and orientation of positive psychology. This element of fortitude is echoed by many others who consider doing good and being a good citizen a clear-cut feature of fortitude that goes beyond just being strong and digging deep into one's capacities. It is a very much a feature of the Budapesti Schindlers that they were doing what was right, but also took risks in the service of others during the most challenging of times.

Resilience and coping are closely linked, with resilience considered as the ability to 'bounce back' despite adversity or setbacks and is generally achieved by having good coping resources. Coping is what demonstrates our capacity to 'bounce back' in a personal sense or as a collective of individuals.

That is why people talk about resilient families, resilient communities, and resilient environments. Coping can be construed as what we *do*—the process; and resilience can be seen as the *outcome*. Resilience comes from the Latin 'salire' to spring up, and 'resilire' meaning to leap or spring back, hence the 'bounce back' concept of resilience.

Some researchers describe resilience as recovery, sustainability, and growth from an individual or from a collectivist perspective which might relate to an organisation, a neighbourhood, a community, a city, a state, or even a nation. Coping skills are very much the building blocks of resilience and fortitude. Refugees who build a successful life in their new communities are certainly demonstrating resilience.

But fortitude has additional dimensions; it is made up of our **values** and **beliefs** as well as our resilient coping skills. That is what the Budapesti Schindlers demonstrated in spades.

Resilience is part of healthy development, and striving for wellbeing and healthy development should contribute to our capacity to be resilient.

Some people talk about resilience like it's a magic bullet; that is too good to be true. How individuals compensate or make good their adverse circumstances may require more than individual capacity, so environments and collectives have an important part to play in recovery. John Donne captured this in the title of his 1624 poem, *No Man is an Island*. Donne himself was a soldier and cleric who refused to give up his Catholicism to bow to the newly established post-Reformation Church of England. His poem captures the essence of our interconnected humanity.

No man is an island,
Entire of itself;
Every man is a piece of the continent,

A part of the main.

If a clod be washed away by the sea,
Europe is the less,
As well as if a promontory were:
As well as if a manor of thy friend's
   Or of thine own were.

Any man's death diminishes me,
Because I am involved in mankind.
And therefore never send to know for whom the bell tolls;
It tolls for thee.

As human beings, we are all connected. As people focus on their survival, it is inevitable that they will do whatever it takes. It's also demonstrably part of our nature that in desperate circumstances we look after each other whilst putting our own lives at risk. Those who survive extraordinary trials are likely to have been influenced by the community around them, particularly those who had hope and belief in their capacities to survive—and in the case of the Budapesti Schindlers, also to help.

'Resilience is in part about putting adversity behind you and getting on with the hustle and bustle of life', wrote positive psychology researcher Raymond Lemay. Lemay reflected on how survivors of the Holocaust often thought of themselves as lucky, and the way that they made successful lives in America. He went on to say that this was testament to the fact that 'Coping is the science of *remarkable people* whereas resilience is the story of how remarkable people can be.' Lemay's remarks could be applied to the Budapesti Schindlers or those who landed in Switzerland or Israel or Australia, or, for that matter, in any other country that would have them. They well may have had good fortune and personal capacities for survival, but beyond their experience of trauma, they were remarkable in terms of being able to move beyond the losses and the horrors, and draw on extraordinary capacities to adjust to new circumstances and build new lives.

The philosophy that underpins my work on coping, resilience and fortitude aligns well with the ideas inherent in the movement of Positive Psychology.

Positive Psychology is a relatively recent phenomenon. In 1989, Martin Seligman, a distinguished psychologist at the University of Pennsylvania, became President of the American Psychological Association. Seligman shifted his focus from depression and learned helplessness (how we become helpless in the face of stress) to one of capacity. This heralded the birth of the contemporary Positive Psychology movement with its emphasis on capacity and potential.

Positive Psychology is the philosophical and psychological orientation that some people adopt intuitively. I sometimes consider that people seem to have a 'positive gene'. Some people have 'positivity' in good supply, and others do not. Psychology tries to teach the latter group how to become more positive, as it is a most helpful resource, not only for surviving but for *thriving* and *doing well in life*.

In order that both adults and children may flourish, Positive Psychology researchers such as Barbara Fredrickson and Marcial Losada articulate that there are four main requirements, namely: goodness, generativity, growth and resilience. Goodness is value-laden, just as philosophy or any other system of thought is.

Here, the implication is that leading a 'good life', doing good deeds and caring for others brings satisfaction. Gratitude features strongly in Positive Psychology in that appreciating what one has brings happiness.

'Generativity' is a term coined in 1950 by Erik Erikson to reflect a concern and guide for the next generation. It is a term that reflects the period of middle adulthood when parents are concerned about their children's future. In broader community terms, it is about sustainability, thinking about what's left behind for future generations. It is, then, about social responsibility.

Growth is readily recognised in children in all facets of development. In adulthood, it is more about stimulation, achievement, and satisfaction.

And finally, resilience is the outcome of how we cope and the subsequent building up of a pool of resources that we can draw upon to face challenges.

***

'When the going gets tough, the tough get going', so the saying goes. Indeed, it is in the most challenging circumstances that our fortitude is tested. There are ways in which our coping capacities are put to the test in our everyday lives through the substantial hardships that might come our way, such as illness, war, floods, fire, grief and losses in general.

'Hope springs eternal in the human breast' wrote Alexander Pope, the English poet, in his 1733 poem, *An Essay on Man*.

In everyday life there are less tangible losses such as failure, setbacks, loss of relationships and so on. They each test our coping skills and our capacity to bounce back. Such events often test our capacity to have faith, love, hope, and an ability to see the future with purpose and meaning whilst retaining compassion and care for others. What is common to those who participate in organised religion, those who have firm spiritual beliefs, or engage in practices such as meditation and mindfulness is that they are generally hopeful of positive outcomes. Clearly, hope played a part in people's survival in the long history of the direst of circumstances.

When researching and writing about the Holocaust, one can't go past reading Viktor Frankl's masterpiece, *Man's Search for Meaning*. Regularly, I revisit that longstanding bestseller that has sold over 15 million copies in 24 languages. It was first published in German in 1946, following World War II, and there is an updated 2011 edition with excerpts from Frankl's letters written in 1945, and several lectures delivered in the United States in the 1980s. It is truly the most inspirational book that I have read. It is the sort of book that if I were only able to take one book when stranded on a desert island, this would be the one that I would choose. Embedded in this slim volume are most contemporary theories of psychology, wisdom, and philosophy—each of which is complemented by Frankl's extensive clinical psychiatric experience.

Frankl, the founder and proponent of Logotherapy, describes his approach briefly in the volume. As a contemporary of Sigmund Freud and Alfred Adler he distinguished his approach from theirs, namely pointing out that Freud highlighted the unconscious and focused on the past and the human drives for achieving pleasure; whilst Adler focused on the will to power and the striving for superiority. Of course, both these therapies have made a contribution, and have had, and *still do* have a following. Some people explore their past and restructure their personalities through a lengthy process of reflection and by gaining insight. Some suppress the trauma of the past, and others are able to reflect and consider how to move forward and live well in the present.

In contrast, Logotherapy is not retrospective and less introspective; rather than focusing on the pleasure principle and power for power's sake, which is destructive, it calls on individuals to find purpose and meaning. Frankl believed in the humanity and goodness of people. He, himself, was a survivor of four Nazi concentration camps, including Auschwitz. He writes about forgiveness and reconciliation; good people can be found everywhere, even in the death camps amongst the inmates, and even amongst some overseers and guards.

Above all else, the Budapesti Schindlers had purpose and meaning in their lives. They were driven by the necessity of rescue and assistance, as are many good people driven today.

Frankl first developed Logotherapy prior to his wartime experience, but he wrote that the experience in the death camps provided ample illustration of the value of the approach. Logotherapy is a meaning-centred therapy with a focus on the future rather than dwelling on the past. It has been called the third Viennese School of Psychotherapy, with 'logos' being a Greek word denoting 'meaning' and through therapy, the therapist is helping others to find purpose and meaning for their human existence. Purpose and meaning are defined as the will to live, the engagement with tasks that are meaningful for the individual, including hobbies, nature, the arts, friendship and love. The survivors of the Holocaust, like my family, have certainly demonstrated the will to live at virtually any cost.

Frankl quotes the philosopher Nietzsche, 'He who has the *why* to live for can bear with almost any *how*.' A quote which comes directly from his experience in the camps, where endurance, or what today we might label as resilience or fortitude, is determined by what is going on in our heads: whether we have a purpose or motivation to do and to live. The intention of doing good for the other is often the driver.

In contrast to purpose and meaning, there is the personal inner vacuum which manifests mainly as an emptiness or boredom—Frankl labels this as an existential vacuum. 'People have enough to live by but nothing to live for; they have the means but not the meaning'.

Frankl values freedom above all else as he describes 'the last of the human freedoms is to be able to choose one's attitude to any given circumstances'. He is also keen to point out that there is no judgement or collective guilt. Personal guilt, like self-blame, is not a helpful strategy, but rather by looking forward rather than backward, we are likely to achieve better outcomes. People have freedom of choice and responsibility for themselves and others, but even in that truth he is not critical of how people behave. Immigrants and refugees are often those who value personal freedom above all else. That indeed was the driver for many like my family to leave Communist Hungary in the late 1940s and beyond, looking *forward* rather than focusing on what has been left behind.

Gratitude, the foundation of Positive Psychology, is very much a hallmark of Frankl's thinking. He acknowledges people's goodness, even when it is a precious commodity and is in short supply. His is a theory of hope and purpose.

A legacy of hope and purpose

When I look back at the story of the Budapesti Schindlers, the common pulse in the veins of all the sometimes vastly disparate men was their capacity to hope and believe that their risk-taking and efforts would have worthwhile outcomes.

Whilst the Budapesti Schindlers had inherent strengths and capabilities to deal with whatever life revealed to them, they were over and above all else, leaders—concerned, compassionate people who took responsibility for others. They lived in the moment, taking care of others, being optimistic that their work was worthwhile and believing that the horrors would come to an end.

The Budapesti Schindlers had qualities, abilities and resources that were extraordinary. Hence, some like Schindler, Lutz and Wallenberg have been recognised as Righteous Among the Nations, whilst many Jewish Schindlers have not received such recognition. Today, there is a movement in Israel to find a way to recognise such heroism, for the likes of Eichel and Farkas.

And as for Kasztner, Porter's comprehensive research has cleared his name in a meticulous, documented manner, so as to convince her readers that he was doing his best under the most difficult of circumstances. However, to some, Rezső Kasztner, like Moshe Krausz, still remains a controversial figure. To Nándor Eichel, who is likely to have worked with him and carefully read the *Új Kelet* reports of the trial, and according to his daughter, had a copy of Braham's book in his home, 'he was just doing his best'.

Each of the Budapesti Schindlers had purpose and meaning in their lives, both for their own survival and in the service of others.

It is the drive to be of service, to help and to do one's best—these were clearly a feature of how my uncle Nándor led his life. Nándor continued to practice medicine in Bondi Junction, Sydney, until a few months before his death on the second day of Passover, 12 April 1998.

∴

And as for those other Budapesti Schindlers, there were many with only a few names surfacing in this book. Some have been lauded, others faintly praised, some still in the shadows, and others remain controversial in some quarters.

Clearly, they were an amazing group of men working in unprecedented circumstances, some with strong egos and strong personalities and others wearing the burden of office with dignity and restraint. There may have been ideological and personality clashes, a hierarchy within the structures where they worked, but what is clear is that in the heat of war, they were cooperating and collaborating on many levels, working towards the same ends, saving lives wherever they could, and risking their own.

And as for silence, it is ever-present in our lives. It can be harnessed for service or abandoned as a resource. There is the silence of the long-distance runner, the writer, and the scholar deep in thought; the swimmer counting the strokes as I do on many a morning as a way of staying in the moment, and as a means to an end. There are those who retreat into silence as a form of meditation and personal growth, or a means to transcend the here and now. And then there is the silence of the listener, where the needs of the other are at the fore.

> The shape of silence
> The shape of silence moves like putty in my hands
> It weaves in and out of life for good or for bad
> When there is time to stand up and be counted silence fails
> When there is grief to be shared an embrace can do when words fail
> When there is a good deed to be known the voice of the other best make it heard
> When there is fear of retribution silence plays its part
> And then there is the silence of peace

A life to live moving forward
Love and gratitude play their part in sustaining purpose and meaning
Blue skies under a golden sun remind us all that tomorrow will come
—Erica Frydenberg

Like many child survivors, I piece together stories as best as I can, drawing on childhood memories, reading the writings of others, and, of course, gleaning meaning from the family silences. The words of Paul Simon and Art Garfunkel seem apt in their famous 1964 song, *The Sound of Silence*. Silence can be a friend, as memories fade with the passing of years and the healing of wounds. But there are history books and perhaps other people, older than me, who can provide eyewitness accounts to help make the corrections. In my research I've attempted to make my own corrections to the silence of history. Or at least pay tribute.

In Nándor's final resting place in Sydney, in the silence of the Jewish burial ground, a small stack of pebbles has piled up over the years, each a symbol of esteem and gratitude for the deceased.

With this book, I place my own pebble and give my thanks.

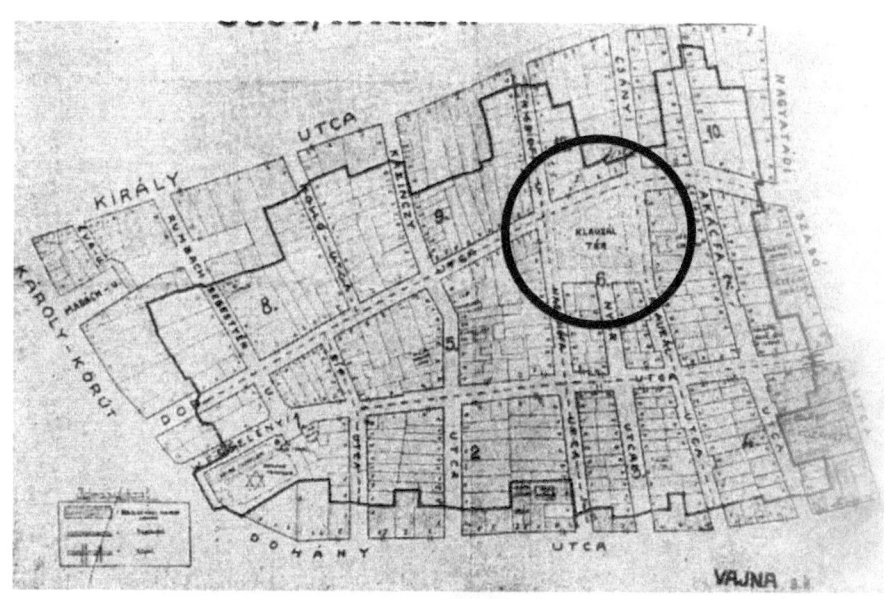

*Area of the Budapest Ghetto by decree, 1944.
My grandparents lived in Klauzál Tér (circled)*

Nefelejcs utca 44-50 (Do Not Forget Me Street)

The Memorial Museum of the Hungarian Speaking Jewry

In the Library, the Museum of Hungarian Speaking Jewry, with Ron Lustig and his mother, Hava, 2023.

Nandor Eichel Budapest Circa 1940

Jewish deportees march through the streets of Kamenets-Podolsk to an execution site outside of the city, 1941. Photo courtesy: United States Holocaust Memorial Museum, courtesy of Ivan Sved

Deportation of the Budapest Jews to the Ghetto. Photo courtesy: Yad Vashem Photo Archive 1544/7

Jews standing in line to receive Swiss letters of protection. The "Glass House", 29 Vadász Street, Budapest, 1944. Photo courtesy: Yad Vashem Photo Archive 1544/7

House of Terror Museum, Budapest

The hastily made yellow star in the Memorial Museum of Hungarian Speaking Jewry

From the top: Masthead Uj Kelet, 1957;
Headline – After the assassination attempt Kasztner felt there was no hope of survival;
Headline – Menkesz denies that he ordered Eckstein to murder Kasztner

The Dohanyi Utca Synagogue, Budapest

Addendum

As you try to assemble the family jigsaw, there remain some missing pieces of the puzzle, even at journey's end. Nevertheless, I have learned a great deal along the way; as much as I know from my study and work in understanding how people cope, situation and context make a difference.

It was 1944. In the chaos of war, the persecution of Jews took place in the beautiful city of Budapest, the centrepiece of Hungary. Time, place and distance may distort events in ways that are hard to gauge, so it is only me as the writer, and you as the reader, doing the best we can to create our own composite of true events.

I read many respected sources in print, some relatively recent publications and some written soon after the events took place last century. It was not always possible to be totally convinced about motives and actions, who had the ideas and who made the right decisions, and who gets credit. Researchers with greater credentials than I have reached differing points of view. And even as one reads texts published close to the events, such as the *Black Book on the Martyrdom of Hungarian Jewry* by Eugene Levai published in 1948, with its extensive clear documentation of reports and transcripts of meetings, it remains for those who were not there to draw conclusions as best as we can without judgement, taking account of the context in which events took place.

When it came to my family, I didn't ultimately discover all of the details I might have wanted to know; however, I can still recognise the value and the wisdom of Nandor's general philosophy and example. As he said of Kasztner, which could also be said of him: he did what he could. He acted with the best judgement as circumstances confronted him. And he retained hope. He set an example of adaptability, resilience, courage and humility that continues to shine for those who remember him, none more respectfully than me. He would have been the first to reject simplistic notions of heroism.

Walking in the shoes of men who did good has been a rewarding experience. Accepting that these less-than-perfect men contributed to serving others—that in itself is worthy of praise and appreciation. We should learn by example and remain humble in the shadow of others who have preceded us.

More than eight decades since World War II came 7 October, 2023, the most horrific episode of the slaughter of Jews in 'modern times', and since the Holocaust. At 6.30 am, more than 1,500 terrorists breached the border fence in Southern Israel as they poured in from Gaza by land and air to make it the deadliest day in Israeli history, killing 1,200 and taking more than 250 men and women and children, including Holocaust survivors, as hostages. The slaughter was accompanied by the violation of women who were terrorised and abused first at a music festival also known as the Nova Festival, near the border with Gaza. From the festival site the terrorists proceeded to kibbutzim—Be'eri and Kfar Aza, and attacked the civilian population there and entered many other communities. The barbarism of the 21st century is as primitive as that of the centuries that came before.

In 2023 there were mobile phones, video recordings and some meticulous interviewing of 150 witnesses and survivors which was reported in the New York Times some three months later. The Spielberg Archives are, for the first time since the aftermath of the Holocaust, once more recording survivor testimonies.

On the eve of December 14th 2025, a father-son duo crossed a footbridge to Bondi Beach in the beautiful harbour city of Sydney to mow people down as they celebrated the Jewish festival of lights, Hanukkah. Fifteen people lost their lives with dozens hospitalised and injured. In the farthermost spot from Europe where the victims of the Holocaust like my family sought refuge, Jew hatred surfaced once more. On this occasion, as before, many heroes emerged. Boris Gurman and his wife Sofia, who tackle the terrorists as they alight from their car, become the first victims to lose their lives. A hero, Ahmed al-Ahmed, jumps on and disarms one of the two gunmen in full view of observers with cameras. He too was among the injured. Many more stories of risk, loss and extraordinary bravery continue to come to light.

On that December day, when my childhood playground became a memorial to terrorism, Australia lost its innocence. The iconic Bondi Beach which represented joy and freedom, the Australian way, the place where I learnt to read, swim and have my first coffee and ride on a Bondi tram.

I have decided to mention these mid twenty-first century atrocities to illustrate how far we have come since man landed on the moon, since technology has linked the world in unimaginable ways, artificial intelligence is set to read our thoughts and emotions and social media on our mobile telecommunication systems has enabled information—true or false—to be circulated around the world in seconds. Despite such impressive advances by humans, the abuse of women and the hatred of Jews has resurfaced once again around the world in heinous, horrific ways.

I have written about good people in bad times, and whilst the Budapesti Schindlers were the group upon which I chose to shine a light, it is time once again to demonstrate concretely, with hard evidence from diverse settings, how brave people can take it upon themselves to do what needs to be done against hatred and persecution.

Chronology
Selectively compiled and adapted from Braham, R. (1993)

1920

September: Adoption of the Law XXV/1920. The so-called 'Numerus Clausus Act'—the first anti-Jewish law in post-World War I Europe, limiting the admission of Jews to institutions of higher learning.

1939

28-29 May: General elections are held in Hungary in which the ultra-rightists (*Nyilas*) parties, which had won only two seats in 1935, now win 49.

1941

27 June: Hungary joins Germany's Third Reich in declaring war against the Soviet Union.

27-28 August: The majority of the 16,000-18,000 'alien' Jews deported from Hungary are slaughtered near Kamenets-Podolsky.

1942

December 2: The Kállay government rejects the German demand for the Final Solution

January 2: Carl Lutz arrives in Budapest.

1943

17 April: Horthy and Hitler meet at Schloss Klessheim.

1944

22 January: President Roosevelt issues Executive Order 9417, establishing the War Refugee Board.

14 March: Josef Winniger, a member of the Budapest branch of the *Abwehr*, informs Rudolf (Rezsö) Kasztner, the Executive Officer of the *Va'ada*, about the impending German occupation of Hungary.

19 March: German forces occupy Hungary.

21 March: A coalition of an eight-member Jewish Council is established under the leadership of Samu Stern, the President of the Jewish Community.

24 March: President Roosevelt warns the Hungarian authorities against taking any harsh measure against the Jews.

29 March: The Sztójay-led Council of Ministers issues a series of anti-Jewish decrees, including the one requiring wearing the Star of David.

3 April: American aircraft bomb Budapest. Eichmann and Péter Hain, the head of the Hungarian Security Police, demand that the Jewish Council provide 500 apartments to compensate the Christian air raid victims.

4 April: Baky chairs meeting with the Ministry of the Interior on the ghettoisation of the Jews. Ministry of the Interior issues decree requiring the registration of Jews. Authorities order the confiscation of 1,500 Jewish apartments to compensate the Christian victims of the 3 April raid.

5 April: Jews begin to wear the yellow star. Kasztner and Joel Brand meet SS member Wisliceny for the first time.

21 April: Kasztner hands over to the SS 2.5 million Pengős as the second instalment relating to an agreement on the 'rescue' of Hungarian Jews. (The first instalment of 3 million Pengős was delivered to Krumey and Hunsche a few days earlier).

25 April: Eichmann summons Brand and makes his 'blood for trucks' offer.

26 April: Dejudification leaders hold meetings.

26 April: Carl Lutz requests emigration permits for 7,000 Jewish persons from the Hungarian Foreign Ministry.

4 May: Wisliceny confidentially informs Kasztner about the decision to totally deport the Jews of Hungary.

15 May: The systematic deportation of Hungarian Jews begins.

17 May: Joel Brand and Bandy (György) Grosz leave on the controversial 'trucks for money' mission.

10 June: In an agreement with Eichmann, 388 Jews are transferred from the Kolozsvár ghetto to Budapest to be included in the Kasztner group.

17 June: The Jews of Budapest begin their relocation to specially designated Yellow-Star houses.

Rescue attempts by neutral States, Sweden and Switzerland, led by mainly Lutz and Wallenberg were started in June/July. Thousands of Jews found shelter in 'protected houses' or in the legations of the neutral powers.

19 June: Miklós Krausz sends an abbreviated version of the *Auschwitz Protocols* together with a report of the fate of the Hungarian Jewry to Switzerland.

25-28 June: Trains leave for Strasshof concentration camp and arrive July 4-5 'Jews on ice' as they wait to continue their journey to freedom.

30 June: King Gustav V of Sweden appeals to Horthy on behalf of the Jews.

30 June: The Kasztner Train leaves Budapest with 1,684 people—first to Bergen-Belson and eventually reaches Switzerland.

7 July: Horthy suspends deportations from Hungary.

8 July: The deportation of the Jews from the communities surrounding Budapest is complete.

9 July: Raoul Wallenberg the Swedish diplomat arrives in Budapest.

12 July: Hungary plans to permit the emigration of 7, 800 Jews. The rest to be deported.

18 July: Kasztner arrested and held incommunicado for nine days.

By end of July 200,000 Jews are herded together in about 2,000 houses distinctly marked with yellow badges. These Jews were to be deported in July/August after the Jews in the provinces were deported.

24 July: The Emigration Department for Foreign Interests of the Swiss Legation is opened in the Glass House.

A certain improvement in conditions felt by Jews in August to September when Horthy sought contact with the Allies.

Andor Schwartz writes that on 7 August hundreds of American bombers fly in the sky—the noise was deafening, and it went on till the end of August.

23 August: Romania extricates itself from the Nazi Alliance.

25 August: The Jews of Budapest according to a rumour are to be deported.

24 August: Eichmann and some of his associates leave Hungary.

15 October: Horthy announces decision to extricate Hungary from the Axis Alliance. Szálasi and the Arrow Cross Party, assisted by the Germans, stage a coup and take power.

17 October: Eichmann and his associates return to Budapest. The yellow badge houses had to be closed down, and the concentration of Jews into two big ghettos begins.

17 October: First Arrow Cross raid on the Glass House. Weiss delayed. Lutz got higher officials to order raiders out.

17 October: Ministry of Foreign Affairs notified the foreign missions that 'Jews with Swedish protective passes (4500), with Palestinian entry visas (7000), with Portuguese temporary passports (698) as well as 100 Jewish employees of the Red Cross are released to the foreign missions. Had to leave by November 15.

19 October: All Jewish men 16 to 60 required to report for 'labour duty'

20 October: All Jewish women 16 to 40 required to report for 'labour duty'.

Late October: The Szálasi government said it would honour earlier pledge to recognise those with foreign passports, and those Jews did not have to report for labour service.

23 October: Schutzbreif = Swiss collective letter applies to those with collective passports.

7 November: Hannah Szenes is executed in a Budapest prison by the *Nyilas*.

8 November: The death marches to Hegyeshalom and the Austrian border begin.

8-15 November: The International Ghetto, safe houses near the Danube, is set up in 72 buildings under Swiss protection in the area around Pozsonyi Street for 15,000 Jewish persons, 4,500 Swedish nationals, 2500 from the Vatican, 700 Portuguese nationals and 7,800 Swiss protected individuals. Very crowded conditions. Repairs e.g. plumbing, and medical care serviced by people from the Glass House.

9 November: The Jews of Budapest are forbidden to leave their homes for three days to enable the authorities to doublecheck compliance with the labour obligations.

10 November: The Swiss Ambassador departs Hungary.

12 November: Jews in possession of protective passes or temporary passports from neutral countries are ordered to relocate to designation 'protected houses'.

17 November: Szálasi reveals a final plan for the solution of the 'Jewish Problem'. Hans Jütner reportedly orders the halting of the death marches.

21 November: Eichmann orders the resumption of the death marches.

28 November: Kasztner departs for Switzerland.

29 November: Budapest Ghetto set up. It had 20,000 residents earlier, now houses 70,000.

2 December: The transfer of the Jews of Budapest to the ghetto is completed.

3 December: The *Nyilas* attack The Columbus Street camp, which was under the protection of the International Red Cross.

4 December: Second raid. The gendarmes attack the Glass House.

7 December: The second group of the Kasztner transport consisting of 1,368 Jews arrives in Switzerland.

10 December: The ghetto of Budapest is surrounded by a fence. The headquarters of the Jewish Council are heavily damaged in an air raid.

10 December: The Arrow Cross Government flees Hungary.

22 December: Meeting in Debrecen, the Provisional National Assembly elects a Provisional National Government.

24 December: Soviet troops begin the siege of Budapest. Eichmann and his colleagues together with many *Nyilas*

Arrow Cross escape from Budapest.

31 December: Arrow Cross attacks the Glass House.

1945

1 January: Arthur Weiss is abducted and killed.

11 January: *Nyilas* gangs massacre the patients, nurses, and physicians in the Maros Street Jewish Hospital in Buda.

14 January: *Nyilas* gangs massacre approximately 150 patients and medical personnel in the Orthodox Jewish Hospital at Városmajor.

16 January: Soviet troops liberate the area of Pest containing the 'International Ghetto'.

17-18 January: Soviet troops complete the liberation of Pest, including the ghetto.

18 January: Hungary signs Armistice Agreement with the Allies.

18 January: Liberation of the Glass House.

25 January: Provisional National Government adopts decree establishing a system of people's tribunals for the trial of war criminals.

17 March: The Provisional National Government adopts decree repealing all anti-Jewish laws and decrees.

4 April: Hungary is free of all *Nyilas* troops.

5 April: Carl Lutz departs Budapest.

22 June: The Budapest Committee of the AJDC is established.

29 October: Trials of the major war criminals begin.

1946-2007

1 February 1946, the Kingdom of Hungary was formally abolished and replaced by the Second Republic of Hungary, with a coalition government dominated by the Hungarian Communist Party. The country was eventually taken over by the Soviet-allied government and it became part of the Eastern Bloc. In 1949, a Soviet-inspired constitution was adopted, and the Hungarian People's Republic was formed.

4 August 1947: Kasztner signs an affidavit in support of Kurt Becher.

1 January 1954: The Grünwald-Kasztner libel suit begins in Jerusalem.

22 June 1955: Judge Benjamin Halevi finds that Kasztner had 'sold his soul to the Devil'.

29 July 1956: The Federal Republic of Germany adopts the Federal Indemnification Law.

4 March 1957: Kasztner is assassinated in Tel Aviv and dies 11 days later.

15-17 January 1958: The Supreme Court of Israel posthumously exonerates Kasztner.

31 May 1962: Following his capture by Mossad agents in Argentina (1960) and a lengthy trial in Jerusalem, Adolf Eichmann is hanged in Ramla prison.

1989-90: The Communist regime of Hungary is replaced by a Democratic parliamentary system.

July 2007: Yad Vashem accepts Kasztner archives.

Glossary

Abwehr: The German counterespionage organisation headed by Admiral Wilhelm Canaris.

AJDC: American Joint Distribution Committee; also known as the American Jewish Joint Distribution Committee, or simply as The Joint or JDC. An American philanthropic organisation dedicated to helping distressed Jews the world over.

Arrow Cross Party: See *Nyilaskeresztes Párt*.

Chassidim: Members of an ultra-Orthodox or religious movement in Judaism. It started in the 1700s in Poland and contemporary Western Ukraine (now Poland) as a spiritual revival movement which spread rapidly in Eastern Europe. The majority of the affiliates of the movement today reside in Israel or in the USA. Yiddish is the language generally spoken by them.

Chevra Kadisha: Jewish ritual burial society.

Dejudification: A term denoting a policy or activity relating to the physical elimination of Jews from a particular area.

Final Solution or Final Solution of the Jewish Question: A Nazi euphemism used in correspondence and other forms of communication, denoting the program relating to the extermination of Jews.

Herut: ('Freedom Movement'): A rightist Israeli political party guided by the Zionist Revisionist views of Vladimir Y. Jabotinsky. The parliamentary heir to the clandestine *Irgun Zvai Leumi* (National Military Organisation), the guerrilla organisation that fought the British troops and Arab militants during the mandate era.

Holocaust: Derived from a Greek word meaning 'burnt offering', it has become the most common word used in English and many other languages to describe the Nazi extermination of Jews. The term 'Holocaust' is sometimes used to refer to the persecution of other groups that the Nazis targeted, especially those targeted on a biological basis, in particular the Roma.

Judenrat: Council of Jewish Elders or Jewish Council: A body appointed by the Nazis to administer Jewish affairs under their supervision.

Kipah: Head covering or skullcap worn by Orthodox Jews.

Knesset: Hebrew for 'assembly'; the Parliament of the State of Israel.

Mapai: The centre labour party of Israel that dominated the government during the first decades of the State's existence.

Mizrachi: A centrist Zionist political party and movement of Orthodox Jews.

Nyilaskeresztes Párt (NYKP): The Arrow Cross Party with Nyilas denoting a member or follower of the right wing ultanationalist movement founded in 1935 and led by Ferenc Szalási before and during World War II.

Protective Pass: See *Schutzpass*.

Schutzpass: Protective pass issued to many Jews in Budapest by legations or embassies of neutral states and by the Nunciature.

Shoah: Hebrew word for 'catastrophe'. The term specifically means the killing of the nearly six million Jews in Europe by Nazi Germany and its collaborators.

Sonderkommando: (German: [ˈzɔndɐkɔˌmando], *special unit*) were work units made up of German Nazi death camp prisoners. They were composed of prisoners, usually Jews, who were forced, on threat of their own deaths, to aid with the disposal of gas chamber victims during the Holocaust. The death-camp *Sonderkommandos*, who were always inmates, were unrelated to the *SS-Sonderkommandos*, which were *ad hoc* units formed from members of various SS offices between 1938 and 1945.

The German term was part of the vague and euphemistic language which the Nazis used to refer to aspects of the Final Solution (e.g., *Einsatzkommando*, 'deployment units').

Yellow Star House: One of a series of buildings in Budapest identified by a yellow star in which thousands of Jews were concentrated in 1944.

Yeshiva: Hebrew for 'sitting': school devoted to the study of the Talmud and rabbinical literature.

Endnotes

Chapter 1

1. *Nefelejcs Utca—Do Not Forget Me Street*. This street was named after the 'forget-me-not' flower. The phrase 'Do not forget me' in Hungarian would be *Ne felejts el*. The word *felejcs* doesn't exist in Hungarian—*Nefelejcs* refers to the forget-me-not flower.
2. Postwar Eichmann escaped to Argentina where he was tracked down and abducted by the Israel intelligence agency, Mossad, in 1960. Following a much-publicised trial in Jerusalem he was found guilty and executed by hanging in 1962.
3. The Romani people are an Indo-Aryan ethnic group who primarily live in Europe. They are often referred to as 'Gypsies', a term that is now considered to be offensive but the Hungarian word *cigány* is still widely used by the general population.
4. From Budapest or associated with Budapest—the *i* suffix is used in Hungarian which was used and is familiar to me from my childhood.

Chapter 3

1. There are many versions of this story but it is considered to be mere legend. Mainstream scholars do not consider that there is a relationship between the Huns and the Hungarians. There are sounder historical and etymological explanations for who were/are the Magyars.

    Magyar: Hungarian—'a Finno-Ugric-speaking people living in large numbers in Hungary; the language of this people, a member of this people'; 'as an adjective, relating to this people'.

    Other explanation:
    Four thousand five hundred years ago, in the Ural homeland, more

precisely beyond the eastern slopes of the Urals, along the Ob River and its tributaries, the easternmost branch of the Finno-Ugric ethnic group, the Ugrians, settled. This group consisted of two closely related peoples, one called the Khanty and the other the Mansi, according to their own names. As the centuries passed, these peoples, who lived mainly from river fishing, slowly moved south, settled in wide plains, and gradually switched to animal husbandry.

The Manysi, who lived further south, became a horse-riding people, and sometime 2,000 years ago, but perhaps as early as 500 years earlier, a large group of them separated and slowly moved away from the others. After a while, this group returned beyond the Urals and began their 1,000-year journey southwest, which ended in the Carpathian Basin.

What did they call themselves at that time? Certainly the same as before: *Manysi*. Only later—how much later, we do not know—did they add the word *erj*, meaning 'man,' to this name, which is still present today as part of our words for 'man' and 'husband'. *Manys-erj* thus meant 'Manysi man,' and self-designations with this structure can be found among many peoples.

Over the centuries, the language of this nomadic people also evolved and developed, undergoing numerous sound changes. Of these, only one change is really important: the consonant combination *nys* first became *dzs*, and then finally *gy*. There is a reliable witness to this: the local Manysi still use the name *anysar* for the wild boar's fearsome tusks, which in the language became: *agyar*.

The conquering ancestors therefore arrived in their new homeland under the name *magyer* or *magyeri*. One of the seven tribes also bore this name. Due to the need for vowel harmony, *magyer* changed in two directions: in the direction of low sounds, it became *magyar*, which then served to name the entire people, while in the direction of high sounds, it became *Megyer*, which has been preserved in the names of settlements founded by the aforementioned tribe, such as *Pócsmegyer, Káposztásmegyer*, and the village of *Megyer* in Veszprém County.

So what kind of people are they? According to their language, they are a people of *Manysi* men. They are the successful descendants of that brave, enterprising little group of people who travelled from the far north to the central regions of Europe and, in the fortunate moments of their history, were able to play the role of a modest middle power, while in the less fortunate centuries they successfully fought for their survival. [personal communication from Gyorgy Nemeth]

2. Treaty of Trianon. The Allies' presentation of their terms for peace with Hungary was delayed first by their reluctance to make a treaty with Béla Kun's Communist regime in that country and subsequently by the obvious instability of the more moderate Hungarian governments that assumed office during the Romanian occupation of Budapest (from August to mid-November 1919). Finally, however, the Allies recognized a new government, and on Jan. 16, 1920, at Neuilly, near Paris, a Hungarian delegation received the draft of a treaty.

3. 'Miklós Horthy's consolidation of power in Hungary followed the upheaval of World War I and the subsequent establishment of a new nation-state. After the fall of the Habsburg Empire, Hungary faced significant internal crises, including economic instability and territorial disputes exacerbated by the Treaty of Trianon, which drastically reduced its size and population. In 1919, Count Mihály Károlyi's government was replaced by a short-lived communist regime led by Béla Kun, which prompted a backlash from conservative factions. Horthy emerged as a key military leader of the counterrevolution, ultimately taking control in November 1919. He was appointed as the temporary regent in 1920, promoting a conservative and

nationalist agenda while balancing the influences of fascist movements. Horthy's regime, marked by autocratic governance and social conservatism, also implemented discriminatory laws against Jews and engaged in violent repression against perceived opponents. His rule, however, brought a degree of stability and economic growth to Hungary during the interwar years, despite increasing authoritarianism. Horthy's alignment with Nazi Germany ultimately led Hungary into the Axis alliance during World War II, culminating in military action against the Soviet Union in 1944.'

—Reproduced from Cox, John K (2023) EBSCO

It was not possible to have a king at that time as the peace treaty signed at the end of the war forbade the Hapsburg dynasty from returning to power.

4. Lévai, Eugene (1948). *Black Book on the Martyrdom of Hungarian Jewry*. Zurich; Central European Times Publishing Company, p 82.
5. Ibid, p. 175.
6. Braham, Randolph L. (2000). *The Politics of Genocide: The Holocaust in Hungary*, Wayne State University Press, p. 573.
7. Ibid, p. 991.
8. Ozsváth, Szuszanna. (2010). *When the Danube Ran Red*, New York: Syracuse University Press. The large river Danube clearly had not turned red, but as Szuszanna Ozsváth, a historian and survivor describes in her book, those parts of the Danube that were visible to her did indeed run red.

Chapter 4

1. The USC Shoah testimony (also known as The Institute of Visual History and Education), formally Survivors of the Shoah Visual History Foundation, founded by Steven Spielberg.
2. There are ongoing debates as to who gets credit for the 15,000–18,000 who were saved due to being diverted to work in Austria between June 25–28,

1944, rather than being sent to Auschwitz. Amongst those claiming credit for successful negotiations and interventions are the Jewish leadership of Budapest and others who consider that Kasztner's relationship with the Nazi Kurt Becher led to the saving of these lives. There was a request for forced workers, forwarded to the SS by the Vienna City Council. It was known as the Goods for Blood deal where Kasztner had offered five million Swiss francs to Eichmann for keeping 100,000 Jews in Hungary. How much money changed hands is not clear. These were considered to be the Jews on Ice whose fate was to be determined when the final bartering was completed. Meanwhile they were to be workers. The big surprise was that the train consisted of entire families—men, women and children, so only one third of the contingent was a true workforce. One historian Paul Sanders claims that it was Kasztner and Hansi Brand who would have been bold enough to face up to Eichmann as there had been bartering and money exchanging hands for these 1,800 persons, with only one third of them likely to be true labourers. Others like Ron Lustig from the Memorial Museum for Hungarian Speaking Jewry in Israel, or Paul Bogdanor do not give Kasztner any credit for such rescue. My extended family certainly does.

3. In the 1994 edition of Braham's book it is note 31 on page 1151. This note is worded a little differently but much the same content directing the reader to Levai's Szürke könyv magyar zsidók megmentéséről (Budapest 1946), p. 185-186.
4. Braham, Randolph L. (2000). *The Politics of Genocide: The Holocaust in Hungary,* Wayne State University Press, p. 89.

Chapter 5

1. Horthy was forced to resign, and he and his family were arrested, removed from power and relocated to Germany after Szálasi came to power on 15th

October 1944. He was held in custody until released by the American troops in May 1945. He went from Germany to Switzerland for a while, and from there to Portugal, after providing evidence for the Ministries' Trial of War Crimes in 1948, Horthy settled and lived out his remaining years in exile in Portugal.

2. Various novels could be listed such as Susan Faludy, *In The Dark Room* or Suzsuzsanna Ozsvath, *When The Danube Ran Red*, Mark Szarvas, *Memento Park* and Roxanne de Bastion, *The Piano Player of Budapest*.
3. Lévai, Eugene (1948). Black Book on the Martyrdom of Hungarian Jewry. Zurich; Central European Times Publishing Company, p. 82.
4. Carl Lutz Foundation Budapest. Glass House Memorial Room. (Translated minutes and documents and testimonials Budapest, 1944), p. 20.
5. Vámos, György. (2012). Carl Lutz (1895-1975). Infolio éditions CH-1124 Gollion pp. 35-36.
6. Porter, Anna. (2008). Kasztner's Train: The True Story of an Unknown Hero of the Holocaust. Australia and New Zealand: Scribe, p. 121.
7. Ibid, p. 164.
8. Vámos, György. (2012). Carl Lutz (1895-1975). Infolio éditions CH-1124 Gollion p. 63.
9. Ibid, p. 69.
10. Weiss's son and wife survived and moved to the US after the war.
11. Vámos, György. (2012). *Carl Lutz (1895-1975)*. Infolio éditions CH-1124 Gollion pp. 105-106.

Chapter 6

1. Illegal financial activities.
2. Porter, Anna. (2008). Kasztner's Train: The True Story of an Unknown Hero of the Holocaust. Australia and New Zealand: Scribe, p. 4.
3. Ibid p. 5.
4. He promoted a political ideology known as Hungarizmus from 1930–

1935 which emerged as a local variant of National Socialism. Led by Ferenc Szálasi, it was an openly irredentist ideology: advocating the restoration to their country of any territory formerly belonging to it, a nationalist and anti-Semitic movement positioned on the right-wing of the Hungarian political spectrum.

5. Porter, Anna. (2008). Kasztner's Train: The True Story of an Unknown Hero of the Holocaust. Australia and New Zealand: Scribe, p. 73.
6. Ibid p. 83.
7. Ibid p. 123.
8. Ibid p. 223.
9. The main personalities of the Va'ada were Ottó Komoly, President; Rezső Kasztner, Executive Vice-President; Samuel Springmann, Treasurer; and Joel Brand, who was in charge of tijul or the underground rescue of Jews. Other members were Hansi Brand (Joel Brand's wife); Ernő Szilágyi from the left-wing Hashomer Hatzair; Peretz Revesz; Andras Biss; and Nison Kahan. After the German occupation in March 1944 responsibilities were split: Ottó Komoly became mainly in charge of dealing with Hungarian government, military and police figures (the so-called 'line A'), while Kasztner (after Brand's departure to Istanbul) led the negotiations with the Germans (the so-called 'line B') including Eichmann. They met at the Café Parisette.
10. Porter, Anna. (2008). Kasztner's Train: The True Story of an Unknown Hero of the Holocaust. Australia and New Zealand: Scribe, p. 247.
11. Ibid p. 248.
12. Rezső Kasztner, "A nagy embervásár" translated to the Great Human Fair, in Porter, Anna. (2008). Kasztner's Train: The True Story of an Unknown Hero of the Holocaust. Australia and New Zealand: Scribe, p. 213.
13. To this day Kasztner remains a controversial figure to many. Books have been written and continue to be written about him, what he did and what he should have done, or did not do. Two highly critical volumes are often

quoted, Ben Hecht's Perfidy, first published in 1961 takes a harsh view both on Kasztner as a flawed individual and the Israeli government of the time, whilst Paul Bogdanor's 2016 publication Kasztner's Crime lays the blame on Kasztner for not warning the Hungarian Jews about their likely fate on those trains that were bound for Auschwitz. Critics like Bogdanor argue that had the Jewish population been forewarned they may not have got on those trains. There are counter arguments which emphasise that Kasztner was not in the position in the Budapest Jewish community to have that sort of influence. His role was limited to the Va'ada. When he was bartering with Eichman for those trains to allow Jews to leave, he was forewarned that there would be no deal if any word got out. Overall, I prefer to draw on the telling of the story by historians of the period, like Randolph Braham or Anna Porter, whose research is based on survivor evidence. Both these authors provide sufficient detail on the printed page for the reader to draw their own conclusion.

Chapter 7

1. Lévai, Jenő. Raoul Wallenberg (1948) translated into English by Frank Vajda in 1989 and reprinted 2022 by Melbourne University Press for White Ant Occasional Publishing.
2. Ibid pp. 169-70.
3. Braham, Randolph L. (2000) The Politics of Genocide: The Holocaust in Hungary, New York. Columbia University Press, p. 1239.
4. Lévai, Jenő. Raoul Wallenberg (1948) translated into English by Frank Vajda in 1989 and reprinted 2022 by Melbourne University Press for White Ant Occasional Publishing, p. 135.

Chapter 8

1. Statistics vary but according to some sources such as World Jewish Congress, 2017, there were approximately 800,000 Jews in Hungary during

the war with only 200,000 surviving the war. There were 200,000 Jews in Budapest before the war (20 per cent of the city's inhabitants). Alternative figures are provided by Vámos, György. (2012). *Carl Lutz (1895-1975)*. Infolio éditions CH-1124 Gollion, p. 24.

Chapter 10

1. In the new State of Israel, with its emphasis on identity and the revival of the Hebrew language it was common for Europeans to shed their European identity, including their names and adopt a Hebrew one.
2. The prosecution, imprisonment and subsequent exoneration of Alfred Dreyfus was a trial known as the Dreyfus Affair. A Jewish French military officer, Alfred Dreyfus, was accused and twice convicted of treason for passing military secrets to the Germans. The case came to divide France between the years 1894–1906 and is considered an example of both a political scandal, and one that reverberated throughout Europe as strongly motivated by antisemitism. It was considered the impetus for Theodore Herzl to seek to establish a homeland for the Jewish people.
3. Porter, Anna. (2008). *Kasztner's Train: The True Story of an Unknown Hero of the Holocaust*. Australia and New Zealand: Scribe, p. 436.
4. Ibid p. 419.
5. Ibid p. 465.
6. Martin Buber, born in Vienna in 1878, died in Jerusalem in 1965. He was nominated for the Nobel Prize in literature 10 times and the Nobel Peace Prize seven times. In 1938 he settled in Jerusalem as a rofessor at the Hebrew University. By 1948 he had become the best-known Israeli philosopher.

Chapter 11

1. Randolph Braham was born to a Jewish family in Bucharest in Romania, in 1922 as Adolf Ábrahám and died in 2018 in Queens, New York City, New York, USA.

Viktor Orban, a Hungarian lawyer and politician who has been the 56th prime minister of Hungary since 2010, previously holding the office from 1998 to 2002, is a controversial leader. Following the escalation of the migrant crisis in Europe in the 2010s, his political party, Fidesz, began using right-wing populist and anti-immigrant rhetoric, but currently is openly supportive of Hungary's Jewish population and Israel.

References

Bogdanor, Paul (2016). *Kasztner's Crime.* Transaction Publishers.

Braham, Randolph L. (1981) *A népirtás politikája* p. 1103 note no. 32.

Braham, Randolph L. (2000) *The Politics of Genocide: The Holocaust in Hungary,* New York. Columbia University Press.

Churchill, W Hansard reference

Encyclopaedia Judaica (2007) Second edition: Thomson Gale, under licence from Keter Publishing.

Hecht, Ben. (1999). *Perfidy... An exploration of the Kastner affair: a conspiracy, a violation of conscience, criminal betrayal.* Jerusalem: Gefen Publishing House.

LeBor, Adam. (2025). *The Last Days of Budapest.* UK: Head of Zeus.

Lévai, Eugene (1948). *Black Book on the Martyrdom of Hungarian Jewry.* Zurich; Central European Times Publishing Company.

Lévai, Jenő. (1946). *Szürke Könyv Magyar Zsidók Megmentéséről* (Budapest 1946), p 18.

Lévai, Jenő. *Raoul Wallenberg* (1948) translated into English by Frank Vajda in 1989 and reprinted 2022 by Melbourne University Press for White Ant Occasional Publishing.

Carl Lutz Foundation Budapest, 1944 Glass House Memorial Room. (translated minutes and documents and testimonials).

Memorial Museum of Hungarian Speaking Jewry. (2021) *Threads of Memory Weave Community.* Safat Israel.

Ozsvath, Zsuzsanna. (2010). *When the Danube Ran Red,* New York: Syracuse University Press.

Porter, Anna. (2008). *Kasztner's Train: The True Story of an Unknown Hero of the Holocaust.*

Schwartz, Andor. (2003). *Living Memory.* Schwarz Publishing.

Vámos, György. (2012). *Carl Lutz (1895-1975)*. Infolio éditions CH-1124 Gollion

Wajnryb, Ruth. *(2001). The Silence.* Allen & Unwin.

Vajda, Frank. (2016). *Saved to Remember: Raoul Wallenberg, Budapest 1944 and After 2016* Monash University Press.

Acknowledgements

When writing about World War II and particularly focusing on the Holocaust in a way that tries to depict history as concise and accessible, it is inevitable that one draws on historical sources that have already communicated through the printed page, on screen or on-line. This was a period when there are no longer those with first-hand accounts to verify facts. Firstly, therefore, my sincere gratitude is extended to the many historians who dedicated so much of their life's work to record history. I drew heavily on many of those sources who focused on the Holocaust period in Hungary, particularly drawing on the works of Randolph Braham, Frank Vajda and Anna Porter. I am deeply indebted to each of them as without their commitment to record historical facts in great depth and detail, this volume would not have been possible. I drew on Anna Porter's work in print and also watched her on screen. László Borhi was another important source when I watched his Webinar on December 12, 2021, about his father's unique experience and what could only be described as miraculous survival at the hands of the Arrow Cross.

Thank you to the founder of the Shoah Foundation archives (more formally known as the Survivors of the Shoah Visual History Foundation), Steven Spielberg, whom I have not had the good fortune to meet personally. I am among those in the world who owe inordinate gratitude for establishing the recording of live testimonials of the Holocaust survivors, and now the survivors of the October 7, 2023 massacre at the Nova Music Festival, and at a number of kibbutzim in Southern Israel.

I drew on two verbatim testimonies which provided irrevocable evidence and meaning as each survivor of those horror times in Budapest 1944-1945 described their lived experience. The first of these was Suzanne Nozick, the mother of Judy Rogers and Tom Gorog who also both gave me their time so generously and assisted with resources whilst they themselves were engaged in recording their own family's journey. The second was the personal account of Suzanne Avidan, mother of Danny Avidan from the Sydney survivor community. Listening to those interviews brings to life uniquely deep perspectives on the survivors' experience. My sincere thanks and appreciation go to both families for leading me to their parents' testimonies.

On several occasions I was drawn to view the documentary film *Killing Kasztner* featuring the Israeli journalist, politician and granddaughter of Rezső Kasztner, Merav Michaeli. Merav interviewed her mother, Kasztner's daughter Zsuzsi, and Kasztner's assassin on screen. That film brought to life the contribution of Kasztner in human terms by family members who believed unconditionally in the contribution of the man in saving untold numbers of lives in the dark days of Eichmann's time in Budapest. That film, like others, helped me to appreciate the world of Kasztner, and the environment in which men like my uncle Nándor Eichel and János Farkas would have been living and working.

When writing a book about one's personal journey and family there are countless family members who have contributed their stories or assisted in my efforts to gather information. None more so than the family Eichel. My cousin Robert assisted in every way possible, as did his sister Judka in Israel. They too were drawing on childhood memories and little documentation. This was assisted by the work undertaken by Dvorah Eichel as part of her roots project in her high school years, and Tamara Eichel, more recently, as an anaesthetist who published in a medical journal the ground-breaking research that Nándor Eichel had submitted as part of his medical studies. I drew on both of these pieces of research.

George Farkas generously shared his father's unique story, his activities with Wallenberg and interactions with Nándor Eichel. My attention was drawn to some media that occurred at the time that his father's story came to light.

The visit to the Memorial Museum of the Hungarian Speaking Jewry in Safed was one of the highlights of my research journey in Israel. Meeting the

Founder of that not-so-well-known Museum, Hava Lustig, and her son Ron who is now the director gave me another level of appreciation of those who devote their life's work to preserving history. The museum is located in Safed, a very beautiful historically significant part of Israel. The scholarship and dedication to treasuring and preserving for future generations the Hungarian experience of the Holocaust was an eyeopener for me. The fate of the Hungarian Jewry and the heroes, mainly unsung, who were part of the rescue is not well understood. In Holocaust museums and Holocaust study, particularly in Melbourne, Australia, where I live and where the greatest number of Holocaust survivors settled outside the large numbers in Israel, the Hungarian experience is not well recognised. May the work of that Museum in Safed continue to educate and celebrate those who have rescued others during times of extreme danger.

The recognition of non-Jews who have rescued Jews has been acknowledged in Jerusalem at Yad Vashem as Righteous Among the Gentiles, but the recognition of Jews who have rescued other Jews is a relatively recent phenomenon. My attention was drawn to what was happening in that regard by Ron Lustig who introduced me to the work of Bnei Brith and the work of Yuval Alpan who made me aware of the *Committee to Recognise the Heroism of Jewish Rescuers During the Holocaust*. That work is ongoing, and I am truly appreciative of the important research that both these men are engaged in.

Yvonne and Peter Halas have been longstanding family friends. Yvonne and I have experienced much of our Australian childhoods in Bondi together. As carefree children and teenagers the family skeletons did not walk visibly from the cupboard until we were well into our adulthood. At that time I became aware of the significance and impact of the Holocaust on our lives. The stories emerged and continue to be shared with students. Peter became a significant part of our family friendship group in his early adulthood when he and Yvonne became a married couple. His family history is highly pertinent to my interest in this volume. The horrendous activities of the Arrow Cross came into sharp personal focus. Whilst at some levels we had lived with these ghosts during the years of friendship, it is in the context of this volume that the clarity and impact hit directly into my consciousness.

Morry Schwartz, a giant of our literary community, who has a commitment to publish and to educate, sometimes in a difficult post October 7th 2023 environment, generously shared resources amongst which were his remarkable father Andor's memoir, written just prior to his 80th birthday. The memories he draws on are so lucid and numerous that they jump out of the page wanting to be read as a memoir as well as a recorder of history. Morry also shared the very precious volume by Eugene (Jenö) Lévai, *Black Book on the Martyrdom of Hungarian Jewry*, edited and translated into English, published in 1948 whilst the events of the recent past were still vivid in Hungarian consciousness.

Quite late in terms of my family history research in 2024 I spoke with Sydney man Danny Avidan, the nephew of Rosie Gluck. He too had known Nándor Eichel well, their family doctor, and considered him to be a friend and hero. It was exciting for me to listen to his mother, Susan Avidan's 1995 testimonial, from the Shoah Foundation archives. The testimonial backed up by Danny's recollections pointed me directly to how the family were saved by Nándor Eichel.

My family visit to Budapest in 2023 provides a backdrop to the research journey. The experience was revelatory as we were able to reflect on the past and appreciate the present. Getting a foothold on history when visiting a beautiful yet significant place is always a great bonus but for me it was also that I needed to be assisted to locate dwellings and people. Our guide on this journey Andrea Medgyesi from the Jewish Visitor's Service in Budapest was most knowledgeable and helpful. A big thank you and admiration for Andrea and her work.

As the manuscript emerged in draft form, friends and colleagues Carmella Prideaux, Sally Leake, Sam Moshinsky and Dr Brian Stagoll generously provided me with feedback.

And in the final prepublication stage the editorial assistance of Sarah Newton-John and Ruth Rosen is greatly appreciated, as is the support, guidance and encouragement from Debbie Lee, principal of Ginninderra Press, to see this project into print.

Writing can be a solitary and isolating undertaking. Liam Pieper's expertise, professional inputs and our on-task conversations made the enterprise enjoyable. I greatly appreciated that we could meet, talk, share insights and I could get assistance from Liam when, and where, I was stuck. Not only is he talented in the writing world but he is also a generous soul and has a wonderful sense of humour which made our working together so smooth, and a total pleasure.

Romy Moshinsky who assisted in the writing of my family memoir Budapest to Bondi, provided helpful insights on ways forward, and Nathan Hollier who saw *Coping in Good Times and Bad* to print contributed significantly as I was working towards publication.

I was introduced to György Németh virtually in mid-2025. His understanding and scholarship relating to the history of the period, and Hungary in general, his reading of the manuscript, sharing of archival resources, insights, corrections and generous helpfulness was beyond measure. I am truly appreciative and only wish we could have met some years earlier when I first embarked on this journey.

And then there is my extraordinary family who came on the journey to Budapest. That experience was forever memorable and my family's contribution to the richness of my life is beyond words. To Harry and my children, Joshua and Lexi, their partners, Amie and Adam and their children, Oscar, Claudia, Luca, Gemma and Blake, my unconditional love and appreciation to each of you. Our families were survivors of the Holocaust. Australia provided the refuge and opportunity for us to not only continue our lives in freedom but gave us the opportunity to thrive. In gratitude we can look back and say thanks to those who helped us along the way. In hope we look forward to continued peace and joy so that the next and future generations should continue to live productive lives in a harmonious community.

About The Author

Erica Frydenberg AM PhD is an educational, clinical and organisational psychologist who has practised extensively in the Australian educational setting. A Principal Research Fellow and Associate Professor in psychology in the Faculty of Education at the University of Melbourne, and an Honorary Fellow of the Australian Psychological Society, Erica is an experienced consultant and keynote presenter. She has published more than 25 books and 150 articles with a core focus on developing resilience, fortitude and wellbeing from early childhood and throughout adulthood in educational, interpersonal and workplace contexts.

www.ingramcontent.com/pod-product-compliance
Lightning Source LLC
Chambersburg PA
CBHW060353080526
44583CB00012B/297